Praying with

Women

of the

Bible

By Elena Bossetti

D0009547

Pauline
BOOKS & MEDIA
Boston

Library of Congress Cataloging-in-Publication Data

Bosetti, Elena.

  [Donne nel popolo di Dio. English]

  Praying with women of the Bible / Elena Bosetti.

     p. cm.

  ISBN 0-8198-5960-5 (pbk.)

  1. Women in the Bible—Prayers and devotions. 2. Bible—Criticism, interpretation, etc. I. Title.

  BS575.B62513 2009

  220.9'2082—dc22

                  2009002077

The Scripture quotations contained herein are from the *New Revised Standard Version Bible: Catholic Edition*, copyright © 1989, 1993, Division of Christian Education of the National Council of the Churches of Christ in the United States of America. Used by permission. All rights reserved.

Texts of the New Testament used in this work are taken from *The New Testament: St. Paul Catholic Edition*, translated by Mark A. Wauck, copyright © 2000 by the Society of St. Paul, Staten Island, New York, and are used by permission. All rights reserved.

Cover design by Rosana Usselmann

Cover photo by Mary Emmanuel Alves, FSP

Translated by by Margaret Joseph Obrovac, FSP, and Mary Martha Ross, FSP

Originally published in Italian under the title *Donne nel popolo di Dio*
Published by Daughters of St. Paul
Original ISBN 88-01-00962-3

Copyright © 2009, Elledici, 10093 Leumann, Torino, Italy

Published by Pauline Books & Media, 50 Saint Paul's Avenue, Boston, MA 02130-3491. www.pauline.org

Printed in the U.S.A.

Pauline Books & Media is the publishing house of the Daughters of St. Paul, an international congregation of women religious serving the Church with the communications media.

1 2 3 4 5 6 7 8 9   13 12 11 10 09

"From those who remain unnamed, to the most revered women in the Bible, Scripture scholar Elena Bosetti draws us to prayer with a celebration of these women's ways of being faithful. Bosetti brings top-notch scholarship to a reader-friendly form that introduces us to the women and their stories, asks us to consider questions that link their stories to our own, and offers a written prayer at the end. Don't make the mistake of thinking this book is just for women. This is a prayer book for the whole people of God."

— TERESA BLYTHE

Author of 50 Ways to Pray: Practices from Many Traditions and Times, *and Director of the Hesychia School of Spiritual Direction at the Redemptorist Renewal Center in Tucson, Arizona*

"In this valuable work Dr. Bosetti lays the scriptural groundwork for a challenging task facing the Church. Using keen scriptural scholarship deftly transposed into pastoral prayer, she opens to us the significance of the women in Scripture. She helps us begin the task of clarifying the distinct role of the feminine, in its own right, in salvation."

— CARLA MAE STREETER, OP

Professor, Aquinas Institute of Theology, St. Louis, Missouri

"Miles beyond other similar resources, *Praying with Women of the Bible* is a treasure and a revelation. Suitable for both individual and group use, this book is a substantive guide with a clear call to discipleship."

— AMY WELBORN

Author, Mary and the Christian Life: Scriptural Reflections on the First Disciple

"When you hear the word woman do you think love — mission — purpose? Sr. Elena Bosetti does! In this book she 'celebrates the marvel of love that is the strength of life,' just as she says the Song of Songs does. With Mary as a special focus, Bosetti reaps the fruitfulness of the stories of women sown in Sacred Scripture; she teaches us, then challenges us! She asks, 'Do I live my daily and ordinary reality as something I must endure, or as a journey of growth in love?' Reading Bosetti separates chaff from wheat boldly. She leaves no excuses: 'If we want to avoid unloading our frustrations onto others, we must cultivate the wonder of life, the marvel of love.'"

— M. JEAN FRISK, STL
*International Marian Research Institute,
Dayton, Ohio*

"Exceptional! Elena Bosetti gives us not just good, sound teaching, but above all, a unique, distinctive, prayerful dialogue with exemplary women of the Old and New Testament. I especially liked the format, where each woman's story is wisely explored in the way of *lectio divina*, involving the whole person in each encounter — the mind, the will, and the heart.

"*Praying with Women of the Bible* holds a special invitation to women to meditate prayerfully on the holiness witnessed by the women of the Bible, with the ultimate goal that what we hear will transform our lives. I echo Bosetti's desire 'that at the dawn of the Third Millennium other women would amaze humanity by recalling "what [Jesus] had said,"' as Saint Luke notes of the women who first reached the empty tomb on Easter morning. With the guidance of Elena Bosetti's expertise, and through the intercession of Mother Mary, the first and trusted disciple, may it be so!"

— MARÍA DE LOURDES RUIZ SCAPERLANDA
Author of The Seeker's Guide to Mary

To my community of Saliceto (Modena);
to the indefatigable Don Dorval;
to my dearest sisters and brothers of
Saint Thérèse of the Child Jesus Parish,
with whom I joyfully shared the Word.

Contents

Part One

WOMEN IN THE OLD TESTAMENT

Part Two

WOMEN IN THE NEW TESTAMENT

Foreword

In an intervention given at the recent Synod of Bishops on "The Word of God in the Life and Mission of the Church," Pope Benedict XVI, while acknowledging the importance of academic exegesis, emphatically reiterated the mandate of the Second Vatican Council's Dogmatic Constitution on Divine Revelation (*Dei Verbum*) that biblical interpretation not neglect the "divine dimension" of the text. Echoing *Dei Verbum*, he went on to describe what this means in the practical order, namely, that the interpreter must bear in mind (1) the unity of the entire Scripture, (2) the living tradition of the whole Church, and (3) the analogy of faith. He could have cited the work of Elena Bosetti—and this book in particular—as an example of biblical interpretation that does all of the above.

Praying with Women of the Bible is "theological exegesis," to use the Pope's phrase, at its best. Bosetti uses all the tools of historical critical analysis, but deftly so that the reader is never in doubt as to where she is going. She retells these well-known stories of women in the Bible, stopping now and again to explain the original sense of a Hebrew word, to describe an ancient and therefore unfamiliar custom, to invite the reader to hear an echo of the Old Testament in a story from the New. She quotes sparingly from scholarly sources and seems to rely on the pithy and often poignant observations of the Church Fathers. But her analysis is never belabored or burdensome. Clearly, it is a means to an end, that is, the actualization of the text in the life of the reader, and that end is always in Bosetti's view. Hence she concludes each chapter with an invitation to prayerful dialogue with the inspired text. But there is something more, and it is more immediately discernible in this book perhaps than in any of her other books. And that is that Bosetti obviously delights in the company of the women about whom she writes. They are not her subject, but her sisters in faith, and she draws the reader very palpably into this family circle which is sometimes called the "communion of saints."

It has been my good fortune to meet Elena Bosetti, not only on the page, but also in person. We met by chance one day at the convent of the Daughters of St. Paul in Boston. Our conversation was wide-ranging and I was left with one lasting impression: Elena Bosetti is a woman of joyful hope. To return to the language of the Pope's intervention, if Bosetti is able in her writing to overcome the "dualism between exegesis and theology" as she does, it is because she has overcome it in her life. And through her writing she encourages her readers to do so as well.

CELIA SIROIS

Introduction

The experience of the resurrection in the primitive community begins with the reawakened memory of its women. When the women reach the sepulcher, early in the morning of the first day after the Sabbath, they do not find Jesus' body. Rather, according to Luke, they find two men in dazzling robes who say, "'Why are you looking for He Who Lives among the dead? He isn't here—he's risen. Remember —he spoke to you when he was still in Galilee.... Then they remembered what he had said..." (Lk 24:6–8).

Their awakened memory of Jesus is the beginning of the Good News, whose first audience was the Lord's disciples: "... and when they returned from the tomb they told all these things to the Eleven and to all the rest" (Lk 24:9).

That same evening, two disciples walking toward Emmaus confide to the mysterious traveler who had questioned them on the road: "Moreover, some women from among us have amazed us" (Lk 24:22).

The Good News announced by the women that morning after the Sabbath was indeed amazing! Would that at the dawn of the third millennium other women would amaze humanity by recalling "what he had said."

With this in mind, this book offers a series of encounters with selected women of the Old Testament and of the New Testament. Though marked by their various historical-cultural conditions, they serve as a sign of God's original plan for man and woman, both of whom he created in his image.

These encounters follow a model of *lectio divina* according to the Way, Truth, and Life method of Blessed James Alberione, founder of the Pauline Family. The first phase (Truth) consists of attentive listening to the word. The second phase (Way) is spent in dialogue and personal comparison of one's life to the word and, if possible, a group sharing on that word. And the third phase (Life) is dedicated to prayer and forming a concrete resolution, a word to live by, so what we have listened to and meditated on will transform our lives. Thus, the whole person is involved: mind, will, and heart.

Accompanying the exposition of the biblical texts are suggestions for deepening the word. These are useful for both group guidance and personal reflection. I suggest beginning each encounter by invoking the Holy Spirit and concluding it with a prayer to Mary, Mother and Disciple of the Lord, the splendid icon of the Church.

Part One

WOMEN IN THE OLD TESTAMENT

Chapter 1

Woman in the Plan of God

⬭ LISTENING

In a spirit of contemplative listening, we place ourselves at the beginning of the Bible, which recounts God's dream for man and woman.

In Genesis 1:26, God expresses the surprising decision to create man-humanity (the Hebrew *adam* is a collective term) in his image and likeness. It is a bold affirmation that illumines the whole account of creation and makes the human being the mirror of God in this world. If the Hebrew people would not sculpt or paint images of God (in keeping with the First Commandment in Ex 20:4), it is because, in the final analysis, God has already left his divine image in the world—an image sculpted in the human person, in male and female form.

> So God created mankind in his image,
> in the image of God he created him;
> male and female he created them. (Gen 1:27; *RSV*)

The Scripture text moves from the singular ("created him") to the plural ("created them"). Man-humanity, created in the image of God, exists in a twofold form: male and female. Male and female participate in an identical and exalted dignity: they are living "images of God." Woman expresses such an image in the "feminine," and thus she constitutes a unique and original "edition" of the divine presence in this world.

Man and woman are the apex of creation:
Woman, the "you" of man

In Genesis, the sacred author describes the man's wonder and enchantment before his companion. The woman is his "you," the only creature able to mirror him, since, like him, she reflects the radiant image of the Eternal One.

The account of Genesis 2 begins by observing the man's solitude. God places the man in the magnificent Garden of Eden and gives him the duty of cultivating and caring for it. The man, therefore, has both life and work, but it is not enough. He lacks a "you," a companion.

Reflecting aloud, the Eternal One makes a fundamental observation: "It is not good that the man should be alone; I will make him a helper as his partner" (Gen 2:18). Isolation is not a good thing. The human person is made for communion.

The Bible wishes to highlight something especially important: the reciprocity of man and woman. For this reason, the creation of the woman is preceded by the man's tentative failure to find reciprocity with the animals, as if delaying the discovery of the helpmate works to underscore her value.

The sacred author imagines a long procession of animals that God himself organizes, bringing to the man "every animal of the field and every bird of the air" (Gen 2:19). It is the man's job to name the animals and so to declare what they mean to him and what "help" they can offer him. All the animals pass before the man "but for the man there was not found a helper as his partner" (Gen 2:20), that is, a helpmate, an equal.

So then, the sacred text continues, the Lord God casts the man into a deep sleep; God takes one of his ribs and encloses its place with flesh. The Lord God forms into a woman the rib he had taken from the man and brings her to him. Then the man says:

> "This at last is bone of my bones
> and flesh of my flesh;
> this one shall be called Woman [*issah*],
> for out of Man [*ish*] this one was taken." (Gen 2:23)

What does this mythic and poetic language mean? The whole account is meant to evoke wonder, to tear away the shade of obviousness from the fact that two sexes exist. Only those whose eyes are capable of seeing with wonder can open their lips to let their hearts sing!

In fact, a song of praise springs from the mouth of the first man when God brings the woman to him. In all probability, we have before us one of the most ancient wedding songs. It testifies to "the joy of the man who finds himself for the first time before a feminine 'you.'"[2] The woman, image of the Eternal One, is the man's reciprocal, his you, and his essential other.

Woman: a helpmate at man's side

But why, when she is created, is the woman taken from the man? Does not the exact opposite happen in the experience of birth? It is "the man" who is taken from the woman. The Bible does not intend to state exactly how things happened. The idea that God formed woman from the man's rib perhaps follows an ancient tradition and suggests an equal helpmate: the rib comes from the upper—"superior"—part of the man's body.

The expression "a similar helper" (in Hebrew *kenegdô*) means literally "what coincides," what lies in complete agreement. God conceives of the woman as the one who will partner with the man not only sexually, but also in all the expressions of existence: in dialogue, understanding, and dedication. Her help is not, therefore, limited to manual work or reproduction, but points much more to an existential help; she becomes a companion for the journey through life.

Where the man is *ish*, the woman is *issah*. It is impossible to adequately translate the play on words in the Hebrew. Suffice it to say that the lexical similarity indicates the relationship between the plan and the life that binds the man and woman in unity.

"Therefore," concludes the sacred author, "a man leaves his father and his mother and clings to his wife, and they become one flesh" (Gen 2:24).

God orchestrates the meeting of man and woman as freedom from isolation and as the great joy of love.

Eve, mother of all the living

We find the name Eve in Genesis 3:20 after the story of the fall. The man calls his wife "Eve," but only after the fall. Just as he had named the animals, he now names his wife. The name Eve, *Hawwah*, is rooted in *hajah*, which means, "to live," and is bound with her call to be "mother of all living" (Gen 3:20).

However, this mother also transmits death. Eve, the first woman, carries within her a conflict we all experience: the tension between companion and beguiler, between "helpmate" and "vulnerable companion" who is exposed to the tempter's seduction. Eve is the mother of the living whom sin has rendered "dead." Yet her name speaks of life and of the wager that life, though marked by death, will one day see full and definitive victory.

Gerhard von Rad writes:

> This naming of the woman by the man can be seen as an act of faith, not faith in the promises, certainly, which were implied in the sentence of punishment, but as an affirmation of life, seen as a great miracle and mystery that the woman's maternity transmits and conserves beyond toil and death.[3]

∞ TOWARD DEEPER LISTENING

Now we enter more deeply into the admirable beginning of divine creation.

The creation accounts described in Genesis proceed according to the perspective of wisdom. According to wisdom theology, even God has his "you," his companion.

At the beginning of creation, God "buys" wisdom. He acts according to the directive given to the one who desires wisdom:

> The beginning of wisdom is this: Get wisdom
> and whatever else you get, get insight. (Prov 4:7)

God even begins his creative activity with a feminine "you"—Lady Wisdom:

> The LORD created me at the beginning of his work, the
> first of his acts of long ago. (Prov 8:22)

According to the Church Fathers, God created the world in the Word, his eternal word and wisdom. Word and Wisdom incarnate! Masculine and feminine. In this way, at the outset of his activity, God formed his family.

∞ BIBLICAL TEXTS

Wonder at creation: Gen 1:26–28, 2:22–23; Ps 8.
Creative Wisdom: Prov 8:22–31; Ps 139, 146, 147.
Salvation and the new creation: Jer 31:22; Isa 45:8–12, 65:17–19; Rev 21:1–5.

⟳ Dialogue and Comparison

We now go from listening to meditation with the help of some questions. We allow ourselves to be personally summoned by the word, and we compare our life to Jesus Christ, the Word of the living God.

1. Our greatest dignity lies in our being images of God. Infidelity has the power to disfigure our resemblance to the divine, but not to destroy it. Such is the dignity of man and woman!

How do I live the theology of creation as wonder and praise for the gift of life?

2. We recall with gratitude all the "helpmates" whom God has placed along our path. We remember the men and women who have helped us, and we bless the Lord for his mercy.

How am I a "helpmate" for those whom I meet?

3. In God's plan, man and woman are equal similar, but different—similar in that they mirror, or face, each other, but different in that they complement each other. Some rabbis explain that one could translate the expression, "a helpmate who faces him," as "counter-help." This similarity/difference opens up two possibilities: the joy of reciprocity and profound agreement, or hostility and violence.

How do I live reciprocity in my family, especially in my relationships with a spouse, children, siblings, and others?

How do I live out the relationship of male-female collaboration in my family, work, and parish environment?

4. The pastoral dimension of Genesis 1:28 could be developed as a call to man and woman to collaborate in "subduing" the earth, which is understood as "lovingly caring" for all God has created. To subdue does not mean to exploit. The human being, crowning of creation, is not called to exploit the earth's resources for his or her own advantage, but to guard the immense patrimony of life that is the universe, to responsibly invest intelligence and physical energies so that the earth may always be more a garden and home for all.

How do I live my relationship with creation?

Do I feel the responsibility to safeguard creation, that environment entrusted by God to humanity?

◌ Prayer

We invoke the gift of wisdom to develop in the fullness of its expression the image of God in us; so we can be "helpmates" for those whom the Lord has placed along our path; to fully live reciprocity.

Father, give me your wisdom so I may contemplate that marvel you brought into existence: me.

Give me your wisdom so I may recognize with joy and gratitude my helpmates, the different "you's" whom you have placed along my path.

Give me your wisdom so I might be, in my own turn, a helpmate to those you entrust to me. Amen.

We make the prayer of Solomon our own:

O God of my ancestors and LORD *of mercy,*
who have made all things by your word,
and by your wisdom have formed humankind
to have dominion over the creatures you have made,
and rule the world in holiness and righteousness,
and pronounce judgment in uprightness of soul,
give me the wisdom that sits by your throne,
and do not reject me from among your servants.
For I am your servant, the son of your serving girl,
a man who is weak and short-lived,
with little understanding of judgment and laws;
for even one who is perfect among human beings
will be regarded as nothing without the wisdom
   that comes from you....
With you is wisdom, she who knows your works
and was present when you made the world;
she understands what is pleasing in your sight
and what is right according to your commandments.
Send her forth from the holy heavens,
and from the throne of your glory send her,
that she may labor at my side,
and that I may learn what is pleasing to you.
(Wis 9:1–6, 9–10)

———•◆•———

Mary is the new Eve, without any trace of sin, the woman in full solidarity with our nature and true mother of the living. We entrust to her intercession our resolution, our concrete pledge, and the word we promise to live by.

Chapter 2

Sarah: Mother of God's People

∞ LISTENING

We introduce our reflection with a beautiful text from the Letter to the Hebrews. In it Abraham and Sarah are presented as our father and mother in the faith:

> Through faith Abraham obeyed when he was called to leave for a place that he would receive as an inheritance. He left without knowing where he was to go. Through faith he sojourned in the promised land as a foreigner, living in tents with Isaac and Jacob—co-heirs of the same promise. For he was looking forward to a city whose foundations were built and formed by God. Through faith Abraham received the power to father children, even though Sarah herself was barren and he was beyond the usual age, because he trusted the One Who made the promise. And so from one man—one who was as good as dead—was born a multitude of descendants, *as numerous as the stars in the sky, as innumerable as the sand on the seashore.*

> They all died in faith without having received what
> was promised, but they had seen it and greeted it far in
> advance and acknowledged that they were foreigners
> and exiles on earth…. (Heb 11:8–13)

After Adam and Eve, Abraham and Sarah are the first
couple that Scripture describes in detail. After the expulsion
of our first parents from the Garden of Eden, we find lists
of genealogies, but no stories of couples. We don't even
know the name of Noah's wife.

Abraham and Sarah signal a new beginning. We are at
the first U-turn of salvation history. They are the couple
God chooses and blesses. They initiate the return to God,
the movement of conversion toward the Lord that expresses
total obedience to his word and unconditional trust in him.

Chapter 12 of Genesis records in an eminent way the
call of Abram. The call is already anticipated in Genesis
11:27–32 in the life-and-death challenge that accompanies
Abram's first migration—his departure for Haran from his
land, Ur of the Chaldeans.

A caravan marked by death

The text introduces Terah's family and Abram's decision
to emigrate:

> Now these are the descendants of Terah. Terah was the
> father of Abram, Nahor, and Haran; and Haran was the
> father of Lot. Haran died before his father Terah in the
> land of his birth, in Ur of the Chaldeans. Abram and
> Nahor took wives; the name of Abram's wife was Sarai,

> and the name of Nahor's wife was Milcah. She was the daughter of Haran the father of Milcah and Iscah. Now Sarai was barren; she had no child.
>
> Terah took his son Abram and his grandson Lot son of Haran, and his daughter-in-law Sarai, his son Abram's wife, and they went out together from Ur of the Chaldeans to go into the land of Canaan; but when they came to Haran, they settled there. (Gen 11:27–32)

Abram and Sarai, therefore, are already inseparable when they leave Ur of the Chaldeans in a caravan marked by death. The leader of the caravan is Abram's father, Terah. He must be about a hundred years old. (According to Genesis 11:26, he became a father at the age of seventy.) More than by age, Terah must feel weighed down with sorrow over of the death of his son, Haran, which he witnessed. The precise reasons for the move are unknown, but the text points out two family members who have had some encounter with death.

One family member is Lot, who reminds Terah of his dead son; the other is Abram, whose future is already dead because his wife Sarai is "barren; she had no child." (We note the repetition of the fact, for emphasis.) Not included among the travelers, however, are Terah's son Nahor and his wife, Milcah, a fertile couple and therefore the only ones, humanly speaking, who have a future open to life. Those who leave with the aged Terah are marked by death. It is a challenge to life.

In reality, this caravan of people opens up a future of salvation for all humanity.

Sarai's charm

Sarai's stunning beauty is proverbial. As the story goes, there is a famine in the land of Canaan, where Abram is sojourning with his flocks. He decides to go to Egypt and along the way, he turns to his wife and reasons:

> "I know well that you are a woman beautiful in appearance; and when the Egyptians see you, they will say, 'This is his wife'; then they will kill me, but they will let you live. Say you are my sister, so that it may go well with me because of you, and that my life may be spared on your account." (Gen 12:11, 12–13)

Abram's use of the word "sister" has a double meaning for the Egyptians: sister and "spouse" (cf. the Song of Songs and Egyptian love songs). The fact is that Abram is treated well by Pharaoh on Sarai's account (see Gen 12:16). Thus emerges the first contrast between Sarai and Eve: although Eve is the cause of evil for Adam, Sarai is the cause of good for Abram.

What was it about Sarai's beauty that is so irresistible? According to Genesis 20 (in which the account of Genesis 12 is repeated), Sarai was ninety years old! What charm could a ninety-year-old woman possess?

Some have read in Sarai's allure an allusion to the irresistible charm of the *election* (both of Israel and of Christ, the "most handsome of men," Ps 45:3). As mother, Sarah incarnates and anticipates the destiny of the Chosen People: going down to Egypt, arousing interest with her irresistible charm, being taken by Pharaoh, but then being freed and given back to her husband. (Abraham, in this case, represents God himself.) As mother, Sarah prefigures the founding of God's people—Israel and the Church.

Sarai's limitations

The Bible does not recount stories of heroes but of real men and women with defects, limitations, and sins. Sarai's limitation is her jealousy. First, she drives her husband toward the slave girl, Hagar, so that he may at least have a son through her. Then, out of jealousy, she turns into a slave driver, mistreating Hagar to the point that Abram is forced to turn Hagar and his son Ishmael out into the wilderness.

Nevertheless, God makes use of this limitation for his plan of salvation. By means of her jealousy, Sarai unknowingly becomes the guardian of the election. In fact, God tells Abraham, "... whatever Sarah says to you, do as she tells you..." (Gen 21:12). Even though it expresses jealousy, God hears Sarai's voice and uses it for his concert of love and gratuitous election.

When God chooses, he inevitably separates: Abram must separate himself from his people, Isaac from Ishmael, and Jacob from Esau. In the same way, the People of God will be separated from all other peoples of the earth.

The smile of Abraham and Sarah

Abram believes the word of the Lord and sets out on his journey with Sarai. But as the years pass, Sarai grows older, her beauty withers, and her womb remains closed.

In Genesis 17, God renews his promise with Abraham: "You shall be the ancestor of a multitude of nations" (v. 4), and he binds this promise to a perennial alliance, an alliance that Abraham and his descendants will bear in their own flesh in the rite of circumcision:

> "As for Sarah your wife, you shall not call her Sarai, but Sarah shall be her name. I will bless her, and moreover I will give you a son by her, I will bless her, and she shall give rise to nations; kings of peoples shall come from her." (Gen 17:15–16)

Here the sacred author surprises us. As noted, Abraham is a man of unconditional faith. He never objects; he is silent and obedient. But now he cannot help laughing, even as he is prostrate on the ground, that is, in adoration of his God. Faith and unbelief exist together:

> Then Abraham fell on his face and laughed, and said to himself, "Can a child be born to a man who is a hundred years old? Can Sarah, who is ninety years old, bear a child?" (Gen 17:17)

The news is so strange, so unheard-of that Abraham immediately intercedes for the son he already has:

> And Abraham said to God, "O that Ishmael might live in your sight!" God said, "No, but your wife Sarah shall bear you a son, and you shall name him Isaac. I will establish my covenant with him as an everlasting covenant for his offspring after him. As for Ishmael, I have heard you; I will bless him and make him fruitful and exceedingly numerous...." (Gen 17:18–20)

Then the scene is repeated with Sarah. One day, at the hottest time of the day, while Abraham is taking a siesta at the entrance of his tent, three men arrive. Abraham welcomes them with exquisite hospitality. He prepares a succulent banquet for them, and while they eat, "he stood by them" (Gen 18:8), like a servant.

The three of them ask, "Where is your wife, Sarah?" Abraham answers, "There, in the tent." At this point, the sacred text changes from the plural to the singular, as if the threesome were becoming one. (The Fathers of the Church see in this an allusion to the unity and trinity of God.) Therefore, the One says to Abraham: "I will surely return to you in due season, and your wife Sarah shall have a son" (Gen 18:10).

Sarah is eavesdropping from within the tent. As she hears those words, a laugh escapes her, but it is a bitter rather than joyful laugh. No sooner does it escape her lips than it settles in her heart. "So Sarah laughed to herself..." (Gen 18:12).

Sarah's laugh is one of total disillusionment; she has lost hope. She and Abraham are very old, and while she laughs, she probably wants to cry. The Lord who reads hearts hears her weary laugh and turns to Abraham with these words:

> "Why did Sarah laugh, and say, 'Shall I indeed bear a child, now that I am old?' Is anything too wonderful for the Lord? At the set time I will return to you, in due season, and Sarah shall have a son." (Gen 18:13–14)

The Lord uses words similar to those spoken by the archangel Gabriel to Mary: *"nothing will be impossible for*

God" (Lk 1:37). As God announces, so he does. The elderly Sarah conceives and bears a son; then her laugh is full and liberating. There issues from her mouth a cry of joy and wonder: "God has brought laughter for me...." With gentle irony, thinking of her once-incredulous laughter, she imagines a collective laugh that spreads wonder all around: "... everyone who hears will laugh with me" (Gen 21:6).

And she says:

> "Who would have ever said to Abraham that Sarah would nurse children? Yet I have borne him a son in his old age." (Gen 21:7)

Abraham names his son Isaac, which means "a joyful laugh."

○○ Toward Deeper Listening

Sarah is the "blessed sterile one," a characteristic we also find in Rebecca, Isaac's wife, and Rachel, the more beloved of Jacob's two wives.

Becoming a mother is a grace invoked humbly in prayer. God is the conqueror of sterility. God has as much power to open the sterile womb as he has to raise the dead (see Rom 4:17–21; Heb 11:19).

○○ Biblical Texts

The sterility-maternity of Rebecca: Gen 25:21.
The sterility-maternity of Rachel, the mother who dies giving birth: Gen 29:31; 30:1–2; 35:16–20.

The sterility-maternity of Anna, the mother of
  the prophet Samuel: 1 Sam 1:4–20.
The sterility-fecundity of Jerusalem and of God's
  people: Isa 54:1–3; Ps 113:9.
The Pauline recasting of Abraham and Sarah:
  Rom 4:18–25; Gal 4:21–31.

∽ Dialogue and Comparison

*We now go from listening to meditation with the help of some
questions. We allow ourselves to be personally summoned by the
word, and we compare our life to Jesus Christ, the Word of the living God.*

1. From Ur of the Chaldeans leaves a caravan of people
marked by death, among whom is the barren Sarah. Yet,
God outlines humanity's new future with these people.

What implications does this event have for my life and
for that of my family and the Church?

Do I believe that God can truly draw life out of situations of death?

2. Like Sarah, we are, by the very fact of our Baptism,
chosen and blessed with every spiritual blessing in Christ
Jesus, a new Abraham and husband of the Church. This
"beauty" of ours does not know the wear and tear of time.

Am I aware of such beauty? How do the gifts of grace
and blessing sustain me in difficulties?

3. Sarah is a woman of limitations, defects, and jealousy.
God is not afraid of our defects. However, God asks for our

faith in order to fulfill his plan of love *through* our very defects: "for nothing will be impossible for God" (Lk 1:37).

In whom do I really believe? In myself, my professional abilities, my work? Or in the Lord?

Do I trust in God?

Do I pray humbly for God's help?

What has my journey in faith been like until now?

Do I live the obedience of faith?

4. Like Sarah's life, our lives can remain sterile for a long time. We can do many things, apply ourselves, work, and organize, but we do not bear fruit in faith. Yet the Lord has moments of birth in store for us sons and daughters, even in our old age. God calls us to generate life.

How do I live the missionary dimension of my faith in the various settings of my life: school, work, or family?

What can cause "sterility" in me: attachment to my habits, fear of not succeeding, half-hearted generosity?

The Lord calls me to be a father or mother. Am I available to give life to others, to give myself to the point of self-sacrifice, like Rachel, the mother who died giving life?

✺ PRAYER

In the light of the Spirit who makes our humanity fruitful, we contemplate the beauty and the limitations of our community and Church. We ask the gift of spiritual paternity and maternity.

We make our own the prayer of Anna, the mother of the prophet Samuel:

My heart exults in the LORD;
my strength is exalted in my God.
My mouth derides my enemies, because I rejoice in
   my victory.

There is no Holy One like the LORD,
no one besides you;
there is no Rock like our God.
Talk no more so very proudly, let no arrogance come
   from your mouth;
For the LORD is a God of knowledge, and by him
   actions are weighed.
The bows of the mighty are broken, but the feeble gird
   on strength.
Those who were full have hired themselves out for bread,
but those who were hungry are fat with spoil.
The barren has borne seven, but she who has many
   children is forlorn.
The LORD kills and brings to life; he brings down
   to Sheol and raises up.
The LORD makes poor and makes rich; he brings low,
   he also exalts.
He raises up the poor from the dust; he lifts the needy
   from the ash heap,
to make them sit with princes and inherit a seat
   of honor. (1 Sam 2:1, 2–8)

We prolong this prayer with our own words, celebrating the power and mercy of God for us.

We entrust to Mary's intercession our resolution and that particular word we promise to live by.

Chapter 3

Miriam: Prophet of the Exodus

In this chapter, we enter the theme of woman and prophecy, which will be developed in our encounters with two women: Miriam, prophet of the Exodus, and, later, Deborah, prophet-judge of the Promised Land.

We invoke the Holy Spirit, who speaks through the prophets, both men and women, so that we can rediscover the prophetic dimension of our Baptism and receive the gift to live it with renewed vigor.

∽ LISTENING

All believers know the importance of Moses' role in the great adventure of the Hebrews' liberation from slavery in Egypt. However, it is not equally recognized that a great woman, his sister Mary, whom we will call by her Hebrew name, Miriam, accompanied the great leader of the Exodus in his marvelous work.

The Bible and ancient Jewish sources reserve particular importance to Miriam. They designate her by the title of prophet and hail her as a genuine leader. Miriam is the charismatic woman who, on the shore of the Red Sea, takes tambourine in hand and exultantly sings the canticle of victory in the Lord's honor, involving the girls and women of her people in her song and dance.

The story of Miriam actually begins many years before. She is barely ten years old when, hidden among the abundant rushes growing along the banks of the Nile, she bravely begins her adventure beside Moses.

The sister who keeps vigil

Scripture does not name the young girl who hides among the rushes of the Nile to see what will happen to her little brother (Ex 2:4). But Jewish tradition does not hesitate to identify her with Miriam. So, from the earliest, Miriam is beside Moses. The one who would one day lead Israel through the waters of the Red Sea is himself "saved from the waters" thanks in great part to his sister.

Miriam guards and keeps vigil like a mother. She stays at some distance, but from a place where she can see, hear, and help her brother. Her willingness to remain near her brother is full of tenderness and responsibility.

The Jewish book of Jubilees adds a lovely detail to the biblical account: "Your mother came at night to nurse you, and during the day Miriam, your sister, protected you from the birds" (47:5).

Miriam keeps vigil because the brother she loves is in that basket. Out of love for him, she exposes her own life to danger. Certainly, it is the Lord, above all, who keeps vigil over that baby; God intervenes and changes adverse circumstances into providential and fortuitous ones. But the Lord's salvific intervention with regard to Moses passes concretely through the actions of three women: his mother's courage, the pity of Pharaoh's daughter, and the enterprising spirit of little Miriam.

The dancing prophet

Around eighty years later, Moses and Miriam are again together on a shore, this time the shore of the Red Sea. The people have just experienced an exceptional event: they have walked on dry ground in the midst of the sea, while the water submerged Pharaoh's chariots and drivers (see Ex 14:21–31). Full of joy, Moses and Miriam offer their song in honor of Yahweh. It is the famous text known as "the Song at the Sea," one of the most ancient pages of Scripture: "Then the prophet Miriam, Aaron's sister, took a tambourine in her hand; and all the women went out after her with tambourines and with dancing" (Ex 15:20). It is Miriam, moreover, who teaches them the refrain, repeated by the entire assembly: "Sing to the LORD for he has triumphed gloriously; horse and rider he has thrown into the sea" (v. 21).

Miriam sings and dances with such enthusiasm she appears to be in the full vigor of her youth, but she is almost ninety years old. This excites the admiration of young and old. Her deep enthusiasm is contagious and carries the entire feminine contingency along. Everyone sings and celebrates the Lord's victory.

Miriam, the prophet, directs the sentiments of exultation to the true Protagonist. This prevents the celebration from degenerating into self-satisfaction. She directs the praise to the Lord, the only One majestic in holiness, the wonder-worker, the only Victorious One.

So many Jewish mothers have delighted in teaching their children the Song of Miriam, canticle of gratuitous and undreamed-of victory and song of freedom.

The prophet, guide on the way

Undoubtedly, it is not enough for the Hebrews to pass through the Red Sea to possess freedom. To live as free men and women it is not enough to defeat the enemy and intone songs of victory. They must learn freedom patiently day after day. In this sense, their forty years' wandering in the desert constitutes a kind of apprenticeship for freedom. The people need to learn how to trust in God even in the midst of adversity, when they lack bread and water. That is not at all easy.

Right on cue, whenever the people lack water or food, they complain and yearn for Egypt. As paradoxical as it seems, slavery gave them a certain sense of security, while freedom carries with it risk and adventure. This context reveals how precious Miriam's charismatic guidance is. She is actively at the side of Moses and Aaron, and she sustains the people with her prophetic charism.

In the Book of Numbers, we find an account that, at first glance, is not flattering to Miriam. It tells of an incident of jealousy. Miriam and Aaron murmur against Moses. Because of this, she is struck with leprosy, paying the consequences for her brother Aaron, who is spared the humiliating punishment because of his priestly dignity. Aaron intercedes for her with Moses, who turns to the Lord: "O God, please heal her" (Num 12:13).

God does heal Miriam, but not for seven days, during which time she remains isolated outside the camp. In the meantime, the nation's march is halted: "…the people did not set out on the march until Miriam had been brought in again" (Num 12:15).

From Jewish tradition, this detail of the community waiting seven days is seen as an external sign of this extraordinary woman's dignity. Miriam's importance is such that *all wait for her:* the people, the priests, and the cloud—that is, God himself. This is how a truly important woman is awaited! And so, conclude the rabbis, Miriam deserves to be "awaited" as a recompense for her having waited on the banks of the Nile so that Moses' life might be saved.

> Miriam waited for one hour … and because of her, God made the Ark and the Shekinah, the priests and the levites and all of Israel, with the cloud of glory, wait in the desert for seven days. [4]

Miriam is truly important; she is a woman who guides the journey (see Mic 6:4). She is important not *because* she had no defects, but rather *notwithstanding* her defects and limitations.

The prophet who provides water

The announcement of Miriam's death is followed with the news that "there was no water for the congregation" (Num 20:2). The sacred text seems to be simply giving one bit of news after another without any relation of cause and effect. But the proximity of the two events impressed the teachers of Israel, who saw a connection: Miriam dies and, as a result, the community goes without water.

This is a symbolic reading. At Miriam's death the well runs dry. This is her prophecy, the water of freedom, and the word of God that she helped to keep alive in the midst of the people.

Miriam spoke in the name of the Lord and waited for his word to be fulfilled. She entrusted herself to the Lord and so permitted the water to spring up from a deep well. The water of the divine word vivified Israel as it journeyed in the desert toward the Promised Land.

⟲ TOWARD DEEPER LISTENING

The most explicit recognition of Miriam's importance comes from the prophet Micah, who numbers her among the marvels accomplished by the Lord:

"…I sent before you Moses,
    Aaron, and Miriam." (Mic 6:4)

A text of the ancient rabbis affirms that Miriam was "sent" above all to instruct the women. We can therefore hail her as the first woman theologian, expert in the word of the Lord, who exercised her ministry on behalf of the women among her people.

She utters her prophecy through music and song, as if to say that the most sublime teaching is that which touches the heart and causes praise to burst forth from it.

◌ BIBLICAL TEXTS

The prophet Miriam awaiting salvation is paralleled in the New Testament by the waiting prophet Anna: Lk 2:36–38.

Miriam "keeps vigil" over Moses as a sister-shepherd. Meditate on Acts 20:28 and 1 Pet 5:2, where shepherding and keeping watch are closely aligned.

The canticle of Mary (Miriam), the sister of Moses, is reprised in the canticle of Mary, the mother of Jesus: Lk 1:46–55.

Consider the prophetic vocation in the Christian community: 1 Pet 2:9–10; 2 Pet 1:16–21.

◌ DIALOGUE AND COMPARISON

We now go from listening to meditation with the help of some questions. We allow ourselves to be personally summoned by the word, and we compare our life to Jesus Christ, the Word of the living God.

1. Miriam is the sister who keeps vigil, but not in an overbearing way. With discretion, she maintains "a certain distance." She keeps watch because she loves.

How do I exercise vigilance over those entrusted to my care: in my family, at school, at work, in volunteer or parish groups, and in my neighborhood?

2. Miriam is full of enthusiasm for the Lord. At ninety, she draws the young into her song and dance. Where does she find such joy and enthusiasm? If we have passion for life, everything becomes a reason for praise and song.

In spite of the difficulties of daily life, do I find in the word of the Lord profound reasons for joy?

Do I live with sentiments of faith, gratitude, and praise in my day-to-day life?

Do I also foster these sentiments in my brothers and sisters?

3. Miriam is not without defects. She, too, falls into the trap of quick and superficial criticism. But her presence is indispensable: without her, the people cannot continue their journey. Miriam is the one who makes water gush forth for the community, that is to say, the word of the Lord and the wisdom that springs from it.

How do I fulfill the prophetic dimension of my Christian life?

How do I bear witness to hope in my home and work environment?

Am I "inside" the problems that afflict society, or am I indifferent to them? Am I committed to justice, above all in relation to the elderly and the most marginalized?

⌒ Prayer

We contemplate God's action in the history of our nation, city, and parish in the course of this past year. We serenely observe our own place in this history, and we ask forgiveness for our omissions.

We pray for the gift of prophecy, the courage to speak and act frankly. We need to rediscover Miriam's gift and help our brothers and sisters to make an "exodus." We ask that Miriam's passion may live in us.

Miriam,
sister who keeps vigil
over endangered life
until danger yields to salvation,
guide of the daughters of Israel
and ardent interpreter of their hearts,
do not die!
You shed tears in song,
with tambourines
you beat out the joy of life,
the alleluia for Yahweh,
who has marvelously triumphed.
Do not die, Miriam!
Do not let us lack the water of your song,
the water of your prophecy.

Do not die, Miriam!
Live in us, who struggle still
through a new exodus.
Live in us, who dream of true freedom,
boundless love,
the undeserved grace, the song, the dance of peace.
Do not die, Miriam,
before pointing out to us
the peaks of the Promised Land!

———•◆•———

We entrust to the Miriam of the new covenant, the Mother of Jesus, our resolution and the word we want to live by.

Chapter 4

Deborah: The Prophet-Judge

When the People of God enter the Promised Land, they find themselves in an environment that makes it difficult for them to obey. They suddenly face the temptations foreseen by Moses: self-sufficiency, the lure of well-being, and a tendency to forget the Lord. "…[A]nd when your herds and flocks have multiplied, and your silver and gold is multiplied, and all that you have is multiplied, then do not exalt yourself, forgetting the LORD your God, who brought you out of the land of Egypt…" (Deut 8:13, 14).

According to the Book of Judges, Moses had good reason to fear. The people forget the Lord and turn their hearts to pagan gods. Thus they experience new forms of oppression. Then they turn once again to the Lord, pleading for liberation. The Lord allows himself to be moved by the people's cry; he listens to their groaning and raises up liberators.

The judges were charismatic figures whom God raised up to reaffirm Israel's destiny. They were rather improvised political-military leaders, "saviors," who coped with politically and socially difficult situations. They usually did not engage in legal or judiciary activity, as their title seems to imply. It applied in one case however: the case of Deborah.

We invoke the Spirit of wisdom, fortitude, and prophecy so we may begin to understand this great womanly figure and receive help to relate her experience to the situations of our own lives.

∽ Listening

It is amazing to find a woman acting as guide for the Chosen People, a woman who assumes the roles of prophet, judge, and warrior, but such is Deborah, "a mother in Israel" (Judg 5:7). She is a woman who does not shine by reflecting a masculine light, as would the wife or sister of a famous man. Rather, she casts her own light, a ray of sunshine, on the Israelites, including the general Barak.

Under Deborah's palm

The Book of Judges introduces Deborah, whose name means "bee," as the wife of Lappidoth (Judg 4:4). Scripture tells us nothing other than his name. He has no particular role to play, while she is famous even before she takes up the reins of government and becomes "mother in Israel," savior of the homeland. She is famous above all as a prophet and wise woman who guides and judges the disputes that arise among the Israelites. Deborah anticipates Solomon: wisdom that establishes justice.

She is an inspired woman, in a relationship of particular intimacy with the Holy One of Israel: she is the prophet, the mouthpiece of God for her people. And the Israelites go in great numbers to consult her. To speak with her, they climb Mount Ephraim, between Ramah and Bethel. She receives them openly, seated under a palm tree that bears her name: the Palm of Deborah.

The palm is a tree full of symbolism; in the ancient East it was a sacred tree, indicating the glory of God. The walls and doors of the Holy of Holies in the Temple of Solomon were decorated with palms (see 1 Kings 6:29–35). And there, in the proximity of the sanctuary of Bethel, under the palm tree, Deborah reveals the glory of God. What she manifests in the complex plots of history is justice and liberation of the oppressed. Under the Palm of Deborah the glory of God illumines daily life.

"If you will go with me, I will go"

Deborah is a bold prophet who is not afraid to confront the powerful. She takes the initiative in summoning the general Barak and proclaims the divine oracle to him: He is to gather 10,000 men and courageously confront the enemy army. Barak hesitates, fearing failure, and offers an ardent request: "If you will go with me, I will go; but if you will not go with me, I will not go" (Judg 4:8).

He secures for himself the opportunity to consult God through the prophet even during the battle, and, above all, he counts on Deborah's charismatic support. She will give courage to an improvised army that must confront Sisera's troops and its powerful weapons (a good 900 war chariots) from the mighty Canaanite city of Hazor.

Deborah accepts to go into battle with Barak; she announces a surprise ending: the palm of victory for having killed Sisera will not go to the general, but the glory will belong to a woman.

And so she is there at Barak's side, at the top of Mount Tabor, certain of divine intervention. It is she who decides the date of the battle (see Judg 4:14). The Lord will go before Barak, just as the Lord went ahead of his people in the Exodus.

Awake, Deborah, and sing your song!

Finally, our prophet, like Miriam on the shore of the Red Sea, sings to God of victory:

> "... [T]o the LORD I will sing,
> I will make melody to the LORD, the God of Israel."
> (Judg 5:3)

On the banks of the Wadi Kishon the great prodigy is repeated. Once again, the God of Israel has overturned destinies: like the Red Sea of the past, the Wadi Kishon has swept away the mighty.

Deborah arises, awakening all her strength and prophetic ardor, and she sings of the admirable victory that she, as champion, witnessed.

> "Awake, awake, Deborah!
> Awake, awake, utter a song!" (Judg 5:12)

Above the victory of the valiant Israelites and Barak, God has marvelously triumphed. Yet, there is something amazing in this victory, something without precedent in the history of Israel: God has acted by a woman's hand!

With acute psychological finesse, Deborah ends her canticle comparing two women: Jael and Sisera's mother. The first is blessed among women for having risked her life clearly and courageously. She is anxious to welcome the enemy general into her tent, and then, while he sleeps, she nails his head to the ground with a tent peg.

Then there is Sisera's mother, watching through the lattice of her window, waiting impatiently for her son's return, almost sensing the danger. Why are they late? Her maids try to calm her: they must be delayed because they are dividing rich spoils: one or two young girls for each warrior, dyed garments, and embroidered finery for the victors' necks. They have no idea that there has arisen in Israel a woman, Deborah, to reawaken dozing consciences and to reestablish justice, to conquer the enemy and to prevent the women of Israel from being humiliated and divided as the spoils of war.

⟳ TOWARD DEEPER LISTENING

Deborah offers her people a honey drawn from many flowers. In her prophetic song, the sweet memory of past exploits fades before the present experience of salvation. Here is the honey of the Promised Land, which Deborah, the bee, has patiently cultivated under her palm tree.

✑ BIBLICAL TEXTS

Deborah is the wise woman who knows how to resolve
disputes and reestablish justice, prefiguring King
Solomon: see 1 Kings 3:16–28.

The word of God is as sweet as honey: Ezek 3:1–3; Ps
19:10–11, 119:103. It is also bitter: Rev 10:8–11.

Deborah sings: "Most blessed of women be Jael…": Judg
5:24. The exclamation is echoed in Elizabeth's greeting: "Blessed are you among women…!": Lk 1:42.

✑ DIALOGUE AND COMPARISON

*We now go from listening to meditation with the help of some
questions. We allow ourselves to be personally summoned by the
word, and we compare our life to Jesus Christ, the Word of the living God.*

1. Deborah is a woman of peace because she reestab-
lishes justice.

How aware am I of my own calling to be a prophet?

In what gestures and choices do I express this call?

Do I place this gift at the service of others, or is it for
my self-affirmation?

2. To be a person of peace does not mean to be all
honey. Deborah, the bee, also had her "sting," which she
used in battle.

Am I a true peacemaker in my daily life?

In what aspect do I feel I need to make a greater commitment to peace?

Do I defend the weak with concrete and consistent choices?

3. Deborah the prophet manifests God's logic in an eminent way. God chooses the weak to confound the strong. Recall times in which the Lord made use of your littleness to do what you would never have imagined doing.

Do I truly rely on the Lord, who chooses the little to confound the powerful?

Do I rely on the power of God, or do I rely on my financial, intellectual, or moral strength?

⬯ PRAYER

We contemplate God who chooses what is small and weak to manifest his power. We also thank him for our weakness.

We pray to grow in obedience of faith and in joy of proclaiming the word of God. We ask for the gift of wisdom and the courage to prophesy, so that we, like Deborah, may be instruments of liberation. We make her song our own:

When locks are long in Israel,
when the people offer themselves willingly—
bless the LORD!

Hear O kings; give ear, O princes;
to the LORD I will sing,
I will make melody to the LORD, the God of Israel.

LORD, when you went out from Seir,
when you marched from the region of Edom,
the earth trembled,

and the heavens poured,
the clouds indeed poured water.

The mountains quaked before the LORD, the One of
Sinai,
before the LORD, the God of Israel.

In the days of Shamgar son of Anath,
in the days of Jael, caravans ceased
and travelers kept to the byways.
The peasantry prospered in Israel,
they grew fat on plunder,
because you arose, Deborah,
arose as a mother in Israel....

Awake, awake, Deborah!
Awake, awake, utter a song! (Judg 5:2–7, 12)

Blessed James Alberione suggested directing the words of Barak and Deborah to Mary:

> Mary, if you come with me, I will go; if you do not come with me, I will not go. I will go to children, youth, and parish work...if you accompany me, Mary; otherwise, I do not feel like going alone. Mary, cover me with your mantle; fill me with faith and courage; put the words on my lips.... So then, Mary will answer: "I will come with you: *ibo quidem tecum.*"[5]

———•◆•———

We entrust to Mary our resolution and that word we will practice in our lives with her help.

Chapter 5

Abigail: The Wise Woman

The last chapter of Proverbs poses an almost embarrassing question: "A capable wife, who can find?" (31:10). This implies such a woman is a rarity and anyone who succeeds in finding one can consider himself very fortunate.

The text continues with deep appreciation for the woman capable of governing her household well. She is valued above precious pearls. Her children rise up and call her blessed, and her husband offers praise in her honor. Nevertheless, the initial question remains embarrassing. Is it that hard to find a strong, capable, and wise woman?

The question betrays a masculine pessimism concerning a woman's abilities and virtues, a pessimism that circulated especially among those devoted to the study of wisdom and of the law. It likewise reflects the attraction of a wise woman. In the wisdom books, acquiring wisdom and acquiring a woman in one's life are parallel expressions:

The beginning of wisdom is this: Get wisdom.... (Prov 4:7)

He who acquires a wife gets his best possession. (Sir 36:29)

At the beginning of his creative activity, God himself "got" wisdom:

The LORD created me at the beginning of his work,
The first of his acts of long ago. (Prov 8:22)

God is the model of the wise man:

God carries out his work with wisdom, almost as if he were taking a wife, and so begins his activity on a solid basis.[6]

We invoke the Spirit of the Lord, the Spirit of wisdom and intelligence; we ask for wisdom of heart.

∞ LISTENING

In the story of David, one page illustrates the importance of encountering Lady Wisdom.

David is a generous man. Even with his enemy, King Saul, in hand, he refuses to do him any harm (see 1 Sam 24, 26). Still, the great David has his shortcomings and petty moments. One of these moments, like an abyss between two magnificent peaks, is described in First Samuel 25. David would have fallen into a dark whirlpool of terrible revenge had he not met a wise woman, Abigail. She reminds him of what his wounded pride had obscured.

Setting the stage: David's exasperation

The story in First Samuel 25 is about a decidedly exasperated David. Our hero needs provisions to feed the hundreds of men who are following him. He leads a wandering existence in the desert of Judea with these men who are ready to defend him from Saul's deception.

He hears that Nabal, a wealthy rancher, is shearing his sheep. David seizes the moment to request his share in provisions based on a so-called right of brotherhood. He justifies this by reasoning that because he and his men have guaranteed protection for Nabal's shepherds, it is now time for Nabal to pay up (see 1 Sam 25:7–9). But Nabal refuses and David feels repulsed and humiliated: "Who is David? Who is the son of Jesse?" exclaims Nabal.

> "There are many servants today who are breaking away from their masters. Shall I take my bread and my water and the meat that I have butchered for my shearers, and give it to men who come from I do not know where?" (1 Sam 25:10–11)

David's reaction is instantaneous and radical: Nabal must die. He gathers his men and sets out, determined to exterminate the ingrate's whole family before dawn.

The meeting with Abigail

The news of this danger reaches the ears of Abigail, Nabal's wife. Without losing time trying to reason with her husband (she knows it would be useless), she quickly prepares a rich assortment of food:

> [T]wo hundred loaves, two skins of wine, five sheep ready dressed, five measures of parched grain, 100 clusters of raisins, and 200 cakes of figs. She loaded them on donkeys and said to her young men, "Go on ahead of me; I am coming after you." (1 Sam 25:18–19)

Abigail is a woman who knows her mind and takes risks. The meeting between David and Abigail is thrown into relief against an austere and evocative background, the desert mountains of Judea. She descends by a hidden path on the back of a donkey. David, on the opposite slope, is irritated and brooding furiously. He repeats his "truth," inflating and enlarging it, almost as if to excuse the action he has already decided to take. He says:

> "Surely it was in vain that I protected all that this fellow has in the wilderness, so that nothing was missed of all that belonged to him; but he has returned me evil for good. God do so to David and more also, if by morning I leave so much as one male of all who belong to him." (1 Sam 25:21–22)

Suddenly Abigail and David come face to face. She quickly jumps from her saddle, prostrates herself on the ground, and speaks to David: "Upon me alone, my lord, be the guilt." Extraordinary! Abigail is the most innocent of all. Why does she take the blame upon herself? "… [P]lease let your servant speak in your ears," the woman continues, "and hear the words of your servant" (1 Sam 25:24). David immediately calms down and begins to listen. The woman continues to speak in a soothing voice. She then blames her husband:

> "My lord, do not take seriously this ill-natured fellow,
> Nabal; for as his name is, so is he; Nabal is his name, and
> folly is with him; but I, your servant, did not see the
> young men of my lord, whom you sent." (1 Sam 25:25)

David grows ever more impressed. Now Abigail can move in for the attack. And she hits the mark:

> "When the LORD has done to my lord according to all
> the good that he has spoken concerning you, and has
> appointed you prince over Israel, my lord shall have not
> cause of grief, or pangs of conscience, for having shed
> blood without cause or for having saved himself." (1
> Sam 25:30, 31)

Abigail teaches David to entrust his cause to God. Saul had obstinately failed to learn this lesson, and David seems about to fall into the same trap, notwithstanding his prior generosity. In fact, he is so obsessed with his wounded pride that he demands justice. Abigail saves him from falling into vengeance, reorienting his heart toward fear of the Lord. David is enchanted with her and exclaims:

> "Blessed be the LORD, the God of Israel, who sent you
> to meet me today! Blessed be your good sense, and
> blessed be you, who have kept me today from blood-
> guilt and from avenging myself by my own hand!" (1
> Sam 25:32, 33)

The wisdom of leaving justice to God

The end of the story shows how God avenges his servant David. Upon returning home, Abigail finds her husband stone drunk and wisely does not waste her breath explaining what has transpired. At daybreak, however, she tells him about his narrow escape with death. Nabal is so shocked that "his heart died within him" (1 Sam 25:37). Ten days later he dies. David then asks Abigail to marry him, and she consents.

This happy conclusion crowns the central message: entrust your cause to God; do not take justice upon yourself. Let God defend your rights. Do not rush him. Confide in his justice. At David's side stood a wise counselor, and her message is always timely.

∞ TOWARD DEEPER LISTENING

There are moments when a generous heart does not suffice. It seems that the offense is too great. We arrogantly feel the need for justice. We reason more or less like David when Nabal offended him: What an ingrate! He repays good with evil. He'll pay for that....

Abigail reminds us of the wisdom of saying no to self-initiated justice, and the wisdom of saying yes to forgiveness.

∞ BIBLICAL TEXTS

Do not nurse hatred in your heart...do not avenge yourself: Lev 19:17–18; Sir 10:6, 28:1–9; Mt 5:21–24.
Love your enemies: Mt 5:43–48; Lk 6:27–35, 23:34; Acts 7:60.

Have confidence in Yahweh, he will free you: Prov
    20:22, 25:21–22; Rom 12:17–21; 1 Pet 3:9.
Abigail reminds us to wait in wisdom for the right
    moment; there is "a time to keep silence, and a
    time to speak": Eccl 3:7.

∞ DIALOGUE AND COMPARISON

*We now go from listening to meditation with the help of some
questions. We allow ourselves to be personally summoned by the
word, and we compare our life to Jesus Christ, the Word of the living God.*

1. Abigail is a wise woman who reminds David of the
strength of love and forgiveness. The first step in this direction calls for the renunciation of every form of revenge.
Abigail teaches us to free ourselves from the "logic" of
"They'll pay for this" and "Just you wait; I'll show you...."

How do I act toward those who treat me unfairly or
wrong me? Do I forgive wrongs, or do I wait for the oppor-
tune moment to take revenge?

Am I able to pray for someone who has done me some
injustice? If I discover feelings of rancor within myself, do
I ask the Lord to heal my heart?

2. Abigail reminds us of the importance of knowing the
best time to speak and act, the wisdom of recognizing that
everything has its time.

Do I recognize this wisdom in myself: Am I able to dis-
cern the right moment and the best way to intervene? Do

I know how to respect God's timing and plans, or do I try to make mine prevail?

Before making an observation or offering criticism of another person, do I recognize the person's situation, or do I just want to unload and speak my "truth"?

With my family, friends, or in my parish, do I carry out the charity of fraternal correction (see Mt 18:15–18)?

3. Abigail is a woman of peace. She is not afraid to risk and take blame upon herself to save a situation. At times it falls on us, at some personal cost, to make peace in our families and communities, or between different groups or organizations.

Am I aware that I bear some guilt in situations in which, to avoid arguments or trouble, I do not intervene to win back a friend, colleague, or family member?

Am I a person of peace and communion, or do I tend to worsen and embitter situations and conflicts?

I recall any situations in which the Lord helped me to be a peacemaker, and I thank him for it.

⬯ PRAYER

We contemplate the work of peace that God has fulfilled in Christ Jesus:

> *For he is our peace.*
> *He has made the two—Jews and Gentiles—one,*
> *and in his flesh he has torn down the dividing wall,*
> *the protective hedge, of enmity.*

He did this by setting aside the Torah
with its commandments and regulations, making peace
by creating one new man in himself out of the two
and reconciling them both to God in one body
by the cross, putting enmity to death by it.
He came and proclaimed the good news of peace
to you who were far off, and peace to those
        who were near,
for through him we both have access in the one Spirit to
the Father. (Eph 2:14–18)

We present to the Lord the conflicts and situations in which hatred and rancor exist. We pray with the words of Psalm 122 for those people and communities that need peace the most:

Pray for the peace of Jerusalem: "May they prosper
        who love you.
Peace be within your walls, and security within
        your towers."
For the sake of my relatives and friends I will say,
        "Peace be within you."
For the sake of the house of the LORD our God,
        I will seek your good (vv. 6–9).

———•◆•———

We entrust to the intercession of Mary, Queen of Wisdom and Peace, our resolution and that word we will practice in our lives with her help.

Chapter 6

Judith: The Woman Who Frees Her People

The history of Israel witnessed such great leaders as Moses, Joshua, and David. Far more surprising in that history are the stories of feminine charm and ability. Such are the cases of Deborah, Abigail, Esther, and Judith.

Judith is the protagonist in a drama set during the reign of Nebuchadnezzar. However, for the readers of the story, it speaks clearly of a situation close to them (cf. Jdt 4:3).

The historical context seems to be the Maccabean revolt: behind Nebuchadnezzar is hidden Antiochus IV Epiphanes, and the unstoppable enemy army stands for the onslaught of Hellenism (see 1 Macc 1:10–14).

Let us invoke the Spirit of the Lord to open our hearts today to listen to the word. May this Spirit help us understand, through the figure of Judith, the value of a maternity that transcends the biological. Judith is a childless widow and yet is hailed as mother of Israel, mother of a people she has regenerated through faith, prayer, and courage.

∽ LISTENING

Our heroine probably never appeared on history's stage. Judith is a symbolic woman; she represents Judea, as the etymology of her name suggests. She is the living image of the authentic Jewish soul. The story of Judith, exquisitely theological, infuses courage in the people who fight for their own identity and reminds them that their strength does not lie in military arms as much as in unconditional trust in the Lord. Just when all seems lost, Israel comes back to life at the hands of a woman! Without a doubt, Judith evokes the image of many real women who, in different times, have saved the People of God.

Nebuchadnezzar, Holofernes, and the city of Bethulia

The narrator of the Book of Judith plays with the contrast in personalities. First, a powerful king, who flaunts his arrogant presumption: this is Nebuchadnezzar. Next is Holofernes, the assertive and unquestioningly obedient general. Their great army advances like a rushing river, sweeping away everything in its path, from Mesopotamia to Arabia, to the cities of the Mediterranean coast, to the land of Israel. Terror spreads in its wake, infecting all the inhabitants of Judea, but fear does not paralyze the people, who pray and fast instead:

> And every man of Israel cried out to God with great fervor, and they humbled themselves with much fasting. They and their wives and their children and their

cattle and every resident alien and hired laborer and purchased slave—they all put sackcloth around their waists. And all the Israelite men, women, and children living at Jerusalem prostrated themselves before the temple and put ashes on their heads and spread out their sackcloth before the Lord. They even draped the altar with sackcloth and cried out in unison, praying fervently to the God of Israel not to allow their infants to be carried off and their wives to be taken as booty, and the towns they had inherited to be destroyed, and the sanctuary to be profaned and desecrated to the malicious joy of the Gentiles.

The Lord heard their prayers and had regard for their distress.... (Jdt 4:9–13)

At this point there appears a mysterious (unknown) city: Bethulia, "house of God." Jerusalem turns to this city for help: Holofernes lays siege to it, and the people of Bethulia fast and pray, apparently without success. The siege is implacable, and after thirty-four days, lack of water forces the city to the brink of surrender. In their desperation, the people cry out to their leaders: Better to end up as slaves of Holofernes than to helplessly watch their children die! Uzziah, the city's ruler, asks them to wait five days more for a divine intervention *in extremis:*

"Courage, my brothers and sisters! Let us hold out for five days more; by that time the Lord our God will turn his mercy to us again, for he will not forsake us utterly. But if these days pass by, and no help comes for us, I will do as you say." (Jdt 7:30–31)

Judith, the widow

Now Judith appears on the scene. The sacred author's portrayal of Judth is completely uncharacteristic of the Jewish ambience of the time. She is a childless widow. Though still young and beautiful, she does not consider another marriage. Her husband, who died shortly after their marriage, left her a considerable fortune, but Judith seems not to give this much importance.

She spends her days in fasting and prayer, secluded in a small room constructed on the terrace of her house, and she uses her goods to benefit the poor. She lives an almost monastic life at a time when maternity in Jewish society was seen as a value that could not be renounced.

She was a countercultural woman, a woman who loved the God of Israel totally. Rather than bearing children, she thought of being a mother to the poor and to all people.

The biblical story highlights the faith of this woman and her ability to guide political leaders who are on a path impervious to genuine faith. As soon as she learns of the ultimatum the leaders have set before the Lord, she sends for two distinguished leaders of the city and welcomes them with words of fire:

> "Who are you…? You cannot … search out God … or comprehend his thought…. For if he does not choose to help us within these five days, he has power to protect us within any time he pleases…." (Jdt 8:12, 14–15)

What theological wisdom and prophetic strength lie in Judith's words! This woman's faith rises like a mountain above the piety and faith of her people. If the five days Uzziah stipulated are a desperate attempt to put pressure on God's heart to save his people, this woman goes further. Judith proclaims the absolute freedom of the Lord: God is God! You don't make deals with him. You need to entrust yourself to him without hesitation. Judith knows unconditional trust, the wisdom of humility learned in prayer.

From prayer to action

But Judith is also a woman of action, who risks her own life for the good of her people. She backs up her words with actions: she will go herself to the enemy camp, and "the Lord will deliver Israel by my hand" (Jdt 8:33). Then Judith prepares for the hour of deliverance by beautifying and adorning herself, but she first prostrates herself on the ground and prays to her God:

> "[Y]ou are the God of the lowly ... upholder of the weak ... savior of those without hope...." (Jdt 9:11)

> "O God, my God, hear me also—a widow." (Jdt 9:4)

When she leaves her house, festively dressed and perfumed, with a tiara on her head, wearing necklaces and other ornaments, her beauty stuns the elders of the city. She is so alluring as to attract the attention "of all the men who might see her" (Jdt 10:4). So begins her adventure.

Before us are Holofernes and Judith, the general completely enslaved to his king, and the woman whose obedience to the Law of God makes her free and resourceful.

Their two worlds, two ways of reasoning, two contrasting wisdoms clash. Judith's is a wisdom that includes astuteness. She hypnotizes Holofernes with her beauty and words. He is so convinced by her speech that he immediately promises to convert to her God (see Jdt 11:23).

What follows is famous. Like a new David, Judith asks the Lord for strength. Then, brandishing a scimitar with a determined hand, she severs the head of Holofernes.

Judith's triumph clearly indicates the kind of reasoning and wisdom that merits success: not a reasoning full of self, but one that relies on human ingenuity while nurturing humility and trust in God. This triumph also underscores the paradoxical way in which God reveals his saving power: "by the hand of a woman." God shows his power through weakness. It is the leitmotif of this and other stories.

Judith, woman of war and peace

From this perspective, it is easy to see how Judith can ultimately describe herself as a woman of peace. She serves God by lifting up the oppressed and crushing the threatening power. For this reason she is a woman who raises song and celebration.

Like Miriam along the shore of the Red Sea and Deborah after routing the enemy—and Mary in her future Magnificat—our heroine directs all glory to the Lord and reveals her fundamental intention for peace:

> "Begin a new song to my God with tambourines,
> Sing to my Lord with cymbals.

> Raise to him a new psalm ...
> For the Lord is a God who crushes wars...."
> (Jdt 16:1–2)

The Church has read the Book of Judith in counterpoint to Genesis. Here is the beautiful and virile woman, the woman-man who crushes the head of the insidious serpent. This woman now proclaims peace, and her people acclaim her:

> You are the glory of Jerusalem, you are the great boast of Israel, you are the great pride of our nation! (Jdt 15:9)

The Church similarly and jubilantly dedicates these words to she who crushed the head of the enemy-serpent, Mary of Nazareth, the true Jewish woman.

∽ Toward Deeper Listening

To anyone acquainted with the Scriptures of Israel, the story of Judith sounds familiar. In fact, it echoes the exploits of Deborah and Jael. Like Deborah, Judith incarnates prophetic power and ancestry over the leaders of the people. She wisely counsels the leaders of Bethulia, as Deborah did Barak.

Judith also resembles Jael, the woman who invites Sisera into his tent to kill him as he sleeps, driving a stake through his head (see Judg 4:21). Judith seduces and conquers the great Holofernes, as Delilah did Samson (see Judg 16:4–18).

⚭ BIBLICAL TEXTS

The book of Judith teaches that the designs of the
   Lord are beyond us: Jdt 8:12–14; think of Job's
   experience: Job 38:2ff.; 42:1–6; and Ps 139.

"You are the God of the lowly": Jdt 9:11; 1 Sam 2:8;
   Ps 116:1–9; Isa 41:13–20.

"O daughter, you are blessed…": Jdt 13:18; Lk 1:42;
   Ps 45:11–16.

⚭ DIALOGUE AND COMPARISON

*We now go from listening to meditation with the help of some
questions. We allow ourselves to be personally summoned by the
word, and we compare our life to Jesus Christ, the Word of the living God.*

1. God puts even the just, his faithful people, to the test.
The perilous circumstance described in the Book of Judith
is not the result of sin, that is, of the disobedience so often
a characteristic in the past. Rather, this time the people are
committed to living in obedience and fidelity to the Lord's
voice. Yet, like Job, they experience the test of suffering
because of their fidelity, because they would not capitulate
to Holofernes.

How do I live my Christian identity in a culture often
at odds with it?

Are my family and parish communities as vigilant and
faithful as the people of the city of Bethulia?

2. Many exegetes have seen in the powerful enemy that threatened the identity of the Jewish people the danger of assimilation into Hellenistic culture, against which the Maccabean revolt arose. Obviously those who conform do not experience opposition and adversity. A Church that meets with society's approval does not suffer persecution. But in this case something worse has already happened—it has betrayed its identity.

What dangers seem to most threaten my Christian identity—a hedonistic culture, wealth, a consumer mentality, individualism, compromising with power, living as if God did not exist?

Do I find that I meet more often with approval or adversity? How do I live either situation?

Is my sense of well-being the result of my conformity to current standards and my reasoning as everyone else does?

How can I live as a Christian, as a "foreigner" in this world, and yet remain engaged in the world?

3. Beautiful, young, wealthy, Judith decides to remain widowed. She renounces children of her own, something entirely foreign to her culture, and totally consecrates her life to the service of God and her people.

How do I live my consecration to God in my vocation?

Does my love for Jesus Christ open me to generous service of others?

Am I capable of self-giving for the good of my community even at the cost of some personal advantage, or "good reputation," or other concern?

◯ PRAYER

We contemplate the action of God, carried out by the hand of a woman in humility and weakness. We make our own the prayer of Judith:

> *[Y]ou are the Lord who crushes wars; the Lord is your name ... your strength does not depend on numbers, nor your might on the powerful. But you are the God of the lowly, helper of the oppressed, upholder of the weak, protector of the forsaken, savior of those without hope. Please, please, God of my father, God of the heritage of Israel, Lord of heaven and earth, Creator of the waters, King of all your creation, hear my prayer!*
>
> *... Let your whole nation and every tribe know and understand that you are God, the God of all power and might, and that there is no other who protects the people of Israel but you alone! (Jdt 9:7, 11–12, 14)*

We close with Judith's prayer of praise:

> *Begin a song to my God with tambourines,*
> *Sing to my Lord with cymbals.*
> *Raise to him a new psalm;*
> *exalt him, and call upon his name.*
> *For the Lord is a God who crushes wars...*
> *O Lord, you are great and glorious,*
> *wonderful in strength, invincible.*
> *Let all your creatures serve you,*
> *for you spoke, and they were made.*
> *You sent forth your spirit, and it formed them;*

there is none that can resist your voice.
For the mountains shall be shaken to their foundations
  with the waters;
before your glance the rocks shall melt like wax.
But to those who fear you
you show mercy. (Jdt 16:1–2, 13–15)

———•◆•———

Through the intercession of Mary, the Judith of the New Covenant, we offer to the Lord the sufferings, the problems, and the hopes of our people.

We entrust to her intercession the resolution we made while we listened to the word and compared ourselves with it. We invoke the gift of persevering love that knows how to resist the enemy's seductions.

Chapter 7

Esther: The Woman Who Reverses Destiny

Like Judith, Esther is striking in her beauty and virtue. She, too, saves her people from destruction. Judith, however, is more of a warrior and strategist; Esther is tender and, according to convention, more feminine. She accomplishes her goal not by wielding a sword, but with the persuasive power of her intercession.

The story of Esther takes us to the sumptuous palaces of the Persian king and gives us an insight into the life of the foreigner, the exile, and the poor. The suffering world of the Jewish Diaspora is written into the story of Esther, the orphan.

We invoke the Spirit of God so that our hearts will be open to listen to his word. May we be given eyes to see the needs of our brothers and sisters, hearts to share in their needs, and great humility, faith, and courage to place ourselves at the service of their liberation.

⌒ LISTENING

The Book of Esther was handed down in both Hebrew and Greek. The Greek version (Septuagint) adds passages to the Hebrew text, similarly recognized by the Catholic Church as inspired. Here we will follow the account according to the order of the Hebrew text, which begins with the solemn banquet organized by King Ahasuerus for all his princes and ministers.

The king glories in showing off to his army of Persia and Media, as well as to the nobles and governors of the provinces, "the great wealth of his kingdom and the splendor and pomp of his majesty for many days..." (Esth 1:4). According to the text the precise number of days is 180!

Yet the king is not content. He immediately organizes another seven-day banquet open to everyone. All the people of Susa from the greatest to the least have access to the royal garden. This is more than simply another banquet; it is intended to be the prolongation and crowning point of the first succession of banquets so as to impress everyone with the king's extreme wealth and generosity toward all. The narrator carefully describes the opulence (see Esth 1:6–7).

Vashti, the feminist

In this heavenly garden within the palace of Ahasuerus, amid the festivities, something completely unheard-of occurs: Vashti, the splendid queen, refuses to make an appearance at the king's banquet. He had kept her as his last great surprise, the marvel of the seventh day. She was to be led in by seven eunuchs, wearing the royal crown on her head, "in order to show the peoples and the officials her beauty" (Esth 1:11). But the queen says no. Not only is it strange, but it is, above all, impudent and reckless to oppose the king's wishes. Vashti is a feminist ahead of her time.

The beautiful Vashti will not yield. She will lose her crown, but not her pride. Perhaps she is tired of all the vanity, of being paraded before the ecstatic eyes of admirers. Or maybe she simply prefers the feminine conversation at the banquet she organizes for women in the king's palace.

The wise men of the court to declare Vashti's actions an outrage that should not go unpunished. The proud queen must be dismissed immediately to keep the danger of a feminist revolution from spreading. Memucan, the wisest of the king's seven counselors, concludes:

> "For this deed of the queen will be made known to all women, causing them to look with contempt on their husbands...." (Esth 1:17)

Dismissing the queen will reestablish order; otherwise, the primacy of man over woman, of a husband over his wife, of the king over the queen, could be threatened.

Esther, the submissive beauty

With the dismissal of Queen Vashti, the search begins for beautiful young women for the king. The woman who most pleases him will be crowned queen. So, from among many women, Esther, too, "was taken" (Esth 2:8). Without revealing her Jewish identity, Esther prepares herself for her decisive encounter with the king. The preparations take twelve months: "six months with oil of myrrh and six months with perfumes and cosmetics..." (Esth 2:12). Each woman then passes a night with the king and in the morning is transferred into the harem—at which point she becomes his property. But a woman does not return to the king unless he calls for her by name (see Esth 2:14). These are the laws in effect at the court of Ahasuerus.

When Esther's turn arrives, she immediately conquers the king. He loves her more than all the other women and makes her queen in Vashti's place. He offers a great banquet and grants a day of rest throughout the whole empire. Order has now been reestablished. Esther is as splendid as Vashti, but unlike her, she is humble and submissive.

Up to this point Esther's role is passive. At first glance, she is simply a feminine object of enjoyment: "she was taken to please." She seems to fulfill her duty by giving pleasure to the king. But the Bible has a surprise for us: Esther pleases another king—her God, who will transform this timid girl, bereft at an early age, into a great protagonist. The moment will come when Esther takes the initiative and succeeds in influencing both kings—the God of Israel and the fearsome Ahasuerus—to favor her people.

The threat of extermination

At Ahasuerus' court is a powerful man, Haman, who hates the Hebrews. Above all he hates Mordecai, Esther's

uncle, a Jew who refuses to prostrate himself whenever
Haman passes, as had been ordered. The man will not conform. Such irreverent diversity is intolerable. He must be
eliminated, along with his entire people. Terribly wounded
in his conceit, Haman approaches the king with these
words:

> "There is a certain people scattered and separated
> among the peoples in all the provinces of your king-
> dom; their laws are different from those of every other
> people, and they do not keep the king's laws, so that it
> is not appropriate for the king to tolerate them. If it
> pleases the king, let a decree be issued for their destruc-
> tion.…" (Esth 3:8–9)

The king consents, and on the thirteenth day of the
month of Nisan, the lot, called the "Pur," is cast to decide
the day and the month in which, throughout the empire,
the extermination of the Jews will take place. Lots fall to
the thirteenth day of Adar, the last month of the year. A
letter is then sent to the 127 provinces of the empire with
the irreversible edict to annihilate on that day "all Jews,
young and old, women and children…" (Esth 3:13).

Esther, the woman who liberates her people

Immediately, there is alarm and great lament in the
citadel of Susa. Mordecai covers himself in sackcloth and
ashes and traverses the city, raising a bitter cry. When news
of Mordecai's actions reaches the palace, Esther sends
clothes to him, but he refuses them. Instead, he informs

her of the threat that hangs over their people and sends word to her through the guard that she should present herself to the king to ask for his favor.

This is not as simple a request as it might appear to us today. According to the law, whoever appeared before the king without being summoned would be put to death. Esther confides to Mordecai that she has not been summoned before the king in thirty days (see Esth 4:11). Yet, if the whole people pray and fast, she will risk it. Here begins Esther's adventure. She who had lived virtually all her life passively and submissively now must take the initiative, risking her own life to intercede for her people's liberation. Mordecai reminds her that it was for this that she had been made queen; that certainly happened by divine purpose.

Thus, while the Hebrew community in the citadel of Susa lives under the constant threat of extermination, Esther humbles herself before the Lord and addresses her trusting prayer to him. It is a very beautiful prayer, grounded totally on confidence in the Lord, reinforced by her experience as an orphan: "…help me, who am alone and have no helper but you" (Esth 14:3).

Then, like Judith, Esther moves from prayer to action. She beautifies herself and appears before the king. In her own way, Esther resembles Vashti in her daring, but her actions are the complete opposite. Without the king having called for her, she dares to appear before him, an action meriting death.

The sacred author tells the story in a captivating way. The lion (the king) is conquered by disarming beauty; the strong one who strikes terror in hearts is subjected by feminine tenderness (see Esth 5:3–5). Overcome by fear, Esther faints. In a poignant scene, the king bounds from his throne, takes into his arms his young beloved, who appears even more beautiful in her swooning pallor, and comforts her with surprising words: " 'What is it, Esther? I am your husband. Take courage; You shall not die....' Then he raised the golden scepter and touched her neck with it, he embraced her, and said, 'Speak to me' " (Esth 15:9, 10, 11).

Then follows an event that shows how during a feast the destiny of death is overturned (see Esth 5:5–8), first of all for Esther, on whom the king's scepter gently rests, and then for all her people. The terrible Haman is compelled to do for Mordecai what he had dreamed of for himself: to clothe him in royal robes, with a crown on his head, and conduct him through the city on the king's horse, accompanied by this proclamation: "Thus shall it be done for the man whom the king wishes to honor" (Esth 6:9). In the end, Haman will hang from the very gallows he had prepared for Mordecai.

The lots *(purim)* are overturned, thanks to the intervention of a woman who trusted completely in the Lord and who willingly risked her own life.

Esther and Moses

Another point to consider is the symbolic link between the feast of Passover and the feast of Purim, between the figures of Moses and Esther.

During the month of Nisan, the Jews celebrate Passover, the great memorial of their liberation from Egypt. Precisely during this month of Nisan, the annihilation of the people at Susa was decreed. The sacred author points out that the king's secretaries issue the edict of extermination on the thirteenth of Nisan, the day on which —at sundown—the paschal lamb is immolated. Paradoxically, the end of Israel is set on the day on which it celebrates the memorial of its liberation.

In that paschal context, the figure of Esther resembles that of Moses: it is she whom God has chosen to overturn the lots *(purim)*, to turn the situation upside down. Now the lots are cast for the thirteenth of Adar, the last month of the Jewish calendar. All the Jews are to be exterminated on that day, from the greatest to the least. Instead, on that day the enemies of the Jews are slain, as happened to Pharaoh and his troops as they try to pass through the Red Sea. In that sense, Jews celebrate the feast of Purim, that is, the upheaval of plans that God accomplished through Esther's intervention.

☜ Toward Deeper Listening

Like Judith, Esther does not have children. This may indicate that the sacred author viewed her, like Judith, in the perspective of a wider maternity. Esther bore the people into a new life, liberating them from destruction.

Esther's Hebrew name, Hadassah, means "myrtle." Esther, instead, is a Persian name, which means "star" (*stareh*) and calls to mind the great goddess Ishtar. But the crown of myrtle, that is to say, victory, comes not from Ishtar or from Marduch (the Persian god to whom the name of Mordecai alludes), but from the God of Israel.

∞ BIBLICAL TEXTS

> Esther, like Daniel, encounters the benevolence of the guards, a sign of the divine protection: Esth 2:9–10; Dan 1:3–9.
>
> Esther is seized with mortal anguish and seeks refuge in the Lord: Esth 14:3ff.; so does the Psalmist: Ps 35; so does Jesus in the Garden of Gethsemane: Mk 14:34–36.
>
> Through Esther, God turns the tables and "vindicated his inheritance": Esth 10:12; confront the upending sung by Hannah: 1 Sam 2:4–8; and by Mary in the Magnificat: Lk 1:46–55.

∞ DIALOGUE AND COMPARISON

We now go from listening to meditation with the help of some questions. We allow ourselves to be personally summoned by the word, and we compare our life to Jesus Christ, the Word of the living God.

1. Though she lives in luxury, Esther does not forget the social conditions and faith of her people. She lives out her favored condition within the framework of faith and soli-

darity. It is God who directs history. If she became queen, it was not for herself, but for the life of her people.

Am I aware of my vocation?

Do I use the gifts I've received egoistically, or do I put them at the service of others, for the liberation of my brothers and sisters?

How would I describe the bond that unites me with other people? Is it one of solidarity, or of apathy and lack of interest?

2. Esther experiences success and admiration. She guards her femininity, beauty, and charm, but she guards more carefully her interior beauty and her relationship with God.

How do I act during positive moments of success, attention from others, and recognition? Do I manage to live these moments with joy and balance, praising the Lord because the gifts I possess are his?

During these moments, do I also cultivate that attractiveness that is worth more in God's eyes—my relationship with him and, consequently, my relationship with others?

3. Esther also experiences the difficulty of taking the initiative against the king's orders. Perhaps her loss of both parents had made her timid and insecure. Nevertheless, Esther does not cling to psychological reasons to defend her fear. Instead, she takes refuge in the Lord and in him finds strength to overcome herself and to be reborn as a daring woman who risks her life for her people. That does

not prevent her from feeling all of her fragility. In fact, looking Ahasuerus in the face is enough for her to lose heart. Yet she will rally and fulfill her mission.

Do I run into difficulties similar to Esther's? How do I go through them? Do I allow my past life to paralyze me? Do I get stuck in a rut? Or do I find in prayer the strength to overcome myself in order to do what is asked of me for the good of the community and the people with whom I live?

Do I ever break the rules of social convention for the good of others—in particular to render justice to the least in society?

✧ PRAYER

We contemplate God's work in Esther and we make her prayer our own.

Esther glorifies God, above all, as her people's only Lord and King; she recognizes his justice and the sin of her people; finally she intercedes for the Lord's mercy: he cannot consent to the destruction of his people without dishonoring himself.

"O my Lord, you only are our king; help me, who am alone and have no helper but you, for my danger is in my hand. Ever since I was born I have heard in the tribe of my family that you, O Lord, took Israel out of all the nations, and our ancestors from among all their forebears, for an everlasting inheritance, and that you did for them all that you promised. And now we have sinned before you, and you

have handed us over to our enemies because we glorified their gods. You are righteous, O Lord!

"O Lord, do not surrender your scepter to what has no being; and do not let them laugh at our downfall; but turn their plan against them, and make an example of him who began this against us. Remember, O Lord; make yourself known in this time of our affliction, and give me courage, O King of the gods and Master of all dominion! Put eloquent speech in my mouth before the lion, and turn his heart to hate the man who is fighting against us, so that there may be an end of him and those who agree with him. But save us by your hand, and help me, who am alone and have no helper but you, O Lord." *(Esth 14:3–7, 11–14)*

———•◆•———

We present to the Lord the needs of our communities and of the universal Church. We also present him with our fears, what instinctively pulls us away from adverse or difficult circumstances, and we ask him for the courage to take initiative in word and action, risking ourselves if the good of our brothers and sisters calls for it.

We entrust to the intercession of Mary, the Esther of the New Covenant, the resolution we make while we listen to the word and compare ourselves with it.

Chapter 8

The Beloved of the Song of Songs

In its freshness, the Song of Solomon, also called the Song of Songs, presents to us God's original plan—the reciprocity of man and woman, which sin, from the beginning, has distorted into the dominion of one over the other. Thus, with the Song of Songs, we ideally go back to the beginning of our journey, to the love song of the first human couple.

The protagonists of the Song of Songs are two young people who share a rural life.

> In contact with God's creation, pristine, as if it had just sprung from his hand, the two young people discover each other as two others once had in the great flow of Love, that divine reality whose presence in the world conquers death. And this discovery springs from their pastoral situation, in direct contact as they are with nature.[7]

We invoke the Spirit of Love who is stronger than death.

⌇ Listening

The lovers of the Song of Songs first appear as a shepherd and shepherdess. The pastoral terminology speaks of their love during its engagement, when passion, search, desire, and encounter—feelings that follow one upon another in an endless cycle—consume them in a rarefied atmosphere at the border between dream and reality.

Draw me after you!

The passage that opens the Song of Songs (1:1–4) is like a musical overture: in itself complete, yet open to further development. The Song of Songs begins with a female soloist, and its theme is one of desire:

> "Let him kiss me with the kisses of his mouth!" (v. 2)

We immediately note that the two mouths have not yet met, but rather they seek each other, yearning for what they do not yet possess. Or perhaps they have already tasted and been conquered by the ineffable flavor and fragrance that has left an irrepressible desire to relive that experience:

> "For your love *(dodêka)* is better than wine...." (v. 2b)

Love, tenderness, and caresses are woven into the symbol of the vine, which is prominently featured in the Bible and in Eastern literature. Verse 3 highlights the "perfume," or olfactory sense. Perfume is of fundamental importance in the East. So the young woman sings that her beloved is really her perfume. There is a play on the words *shem* (name) and *shemen* (perfume). His presence is my perfume!

"Draw me [ravish me!] after you, let us make haste."
(v. 4)

The young woman expresses her desire to be introduced into the wedding chamber, into the alcove of the shepherd-king in order to rejoice and celebrate, to taste ("recall") his tenderness. The text expresses a strong desire for intimacy and moves her to another level. In fact, the word *hadar*, which is translated as alcove, literally means "the inner chambers" (perhaps an allusion to the Temple's inner room, the Holy of Holies). The merrymaking is at the same time "a remembering," a celebration. Take me—the young lover seems to say—where I can memorialize our love story. Give me what you have already let me taste! At this point, there is a move from "I" to "we": "I am in love with you!" Love is contagious.

Tell me where you pasture your flock

In Song of Songs 1:5–8, the woman's self-portrait is framed in a pastoral setting. We picture her in the foreground and the daughters of Jerusalem (the chorus) in the background. She presents herself to her friends, speaking of her appearance (she is black and beautiful), and her love story (she did not know how to guard her vineyard). But in verse 7 the discourse changes direction—from the plural to the singular. While speaking to her friends, the young woman directly addresses her beloved as if he were there. Only the *daughters* (plural) of Jerusalem are there, but she addresses her beloved in the first person singular:

"Tell me, you whom my soul loves,
where you pasture your flock...."

The response comes, in fact, from the chorus: "...follow the tracks of the flock..." (Song 1:7–8).

Let's try to expand on the various elements.

- ◆ The scene: It is noon and sunny, and the heat could possibly go to one's head.
- ◆ On the Bedouins' hot tracks is a woman.
- ◆ The woman is dark and beautiful. Her beauty harmonizes with her pastoral surroundings. Her dark skin is the result of her constant exposure to the sun, so hers is an everyday, unsophisticated beauty.
- ◆ Her brothers' useless attempts to control, oppose her. Though young, she has the courage of autonomy.
- ◆ The woman invokes her lover: "Tell me ... where you pasture your flock!"
- ◆ Finally, the chorus indicates the sure path for her search: "follow the tracks of the flock."

And by those tracks the shepherd is discovered.

Love is already described as a continuous search, requiring patience to follow the signs: not the shepherd's footprints directly, but those of his flock. It is a mediated search in the conviction that where the flock is found, so is found the shepherd.

My beloved is mine and I am his

We stop at Song of Songs 2:8–17, which immediately follows the "rendezvous duet" (see 1:9–2:7), the ecstatic

song of two lovers embracing without shame (as in the
Garden of Eden). It is a duet without false modesty and
that resorts to the most ardent images to describe the
attractiveness of the person loved. This time the man
begins, but the woman has the last word:

> "I adjure you, O daughters of Jerusalem ...
> do not stir up or awaken love
> until it is ready!" (Song 2:7)

Song of Songs 2:8–17 envelopes us in a stupendous
springtime scene. Again, the woman takes the initiative.
Note the growing tension:

- the voice;
- the steps;
- the eyes;
- "our wall" of encounter that now obstructs her view
  because he is on the other side;
- and again, the voice now recognizable, speaking
  words dreamed-of and invoked.

She had pleaded, "Ravish me!" (Song 1:4). He tells her,
"Come away!" Run away with me! Here is perfect correspon-
dence between the woman who sees her beloved through the
lattice and the man who sees his beloved like a dove in the
clefts of the rock. In sequence: face, voice; voice, face.

According to some exegetes, the little foxes mentioned
in 2:15 may be jackal pups, greedy for the ripening grapes.
However, given the symbolism of the vine as the feminine
physique, the little foxes may be understood as whatever
waits for love in its integrity.

The woman of the Song of Songs reasserts her fidelity and desire for her beloved:

> "My beloved is mine and I am his;
> he pastures his flock among the lilies." (Song 2:16)

She expresses mutual belonging, spousal alliance, a song of the ineffable joy of this reciprocal belonging.

Toward a love that never fades

In Song of Songs 7:11–8:7 we again take up the elements already noted and gathered in a sublime spiral in which the woman no longer experiences the man's dominion, but the joy of his passionate desire. The norm in Genesis 3:16 is inverted. Whereas Genesis 3:16 attests to the coexistence of attraction and domination: "… your desire shall be for your husband, and he shall rule over you," in Song of Songs 7:10 the woman, using the same words, upends the situation: "I am my beloved's, and his desire is for me."

Between the two lovers of the Song of Songs, there is total reciprocity and no dominance, violence, or oppression of one over the other. The woman asks her beloved to place her as a perennial sign of love on his heart and arm, so that even at times of absence and inevitable separation, they will be bound by the memory of their love and their desire to be reunited:

> Set me as a seal upon your heart,
> as a seal upon your arm;
> for love is strong as death,
> passion fierce as the grave.

Its flashes are flashes of fire, a raging flame.
Many waters cannot quench love,
neither can floods drown it.
If one offered for love
all the wealth of his house,
it would be utterly scorned. (Song 8:6–7)

Our thoughts run to the Book of Revelation, to the final wedding feast of the Spouse and the Lamb. But this text incites us to live our present life more radically as a question of love, as did Christ, who tenderly loves his Church and gave himself entirely for her (see Eph 5:25).

⌒ TOWARD DEEPER LISTENING

Pastoral terminology and the terminology of love—not the first time we have encountered such a union of terms. Love, care, and mercy constitute the unexpressed content of shepherding language when it refers to God as well as to the human leaders of the people. In the Song of Songs, however, it reaches an unprecedented depth of meaning, bound up in the context in which that language is used. It is like the world of children who discover life's horizon for the first time with new freshness and unparalleled depth.

⌒ BIBLICAL TEXTS

The beloved is a shepherd: see Ps 23 and Jn 10 in relation to these passages from the Song of Songs: 1:7–8; 2:16; 6:2–3.

The beloved of the Song of Songs searches for her love in the night and recognizes his voice; so does Mary of Magdalene according to Jn 20:11–16.

The seal on the heart is the sign of a perennial alliance, the sign of fidelity: Deut 6:6–8; Hos 2:21–22; Jer 31:33; Prov 3:3.

☜ Dialogue and Comparison

We now go from listening to meditation with the help of some questions. We allow ourselves to be personally summoned by the word, and we compare our life to Jesus Christ, the Word of the living God.

1. The Song of Songs celebrates the marvel of love that is the strength of life. If we want to avoid unloading our frustrations onto others, we must cultivate the wonder of life, the marvel of love.

How do I cultivate sentiments of wonder and gratitude in my life?

How do I relate to nature?

How do I foster friendships?

2. The young woman of the Song of Songs presents herself as an everyday beauty, blackened by the sun, and, above all, in love. We recall the courage needed to leave our families in order to form new ones, to say yes to a commitment of solidarity and sharing.

Do I still have the ideals and enthusiasm I had when I first made my choice?

Do I live my daily and ordinary reality as something I must endure or as a journey of growth in love?

3. Pastoral service is a matter of love and requires Gospel vigilance, purity of heart, and simplicity in relationships. We confront these attitudes taking direction from the Song of Songs, with particular attention to what risks seem irrelevant and unimportant. The image of the little foxes is always appropriate for an examination of conscience.

What threatens the fidelity of my love and my dedication to the service of my brothers and sisters?

Can I name some "little foxes" in my everyday life that can poison love?

Am I overly curious, watching too much television, having little self-control over my eyes?

Am I unable to hold my tongue?

Am I obsessed with news, food, or success?

☙ Prayer

We contemplate the great love of God for humanity and the love of Christ for his Church and for each of us: He "loved me and gave himself up for me" (Gal 2:20). Saint Teresa of Avila writes:

> My Jesus!... Who can guess how advantageous it is to throw ourselves into the arms of God and establish this pact with His Majesty: I will take care of my Beloved, and my Beloved will take care of me; he will watch over my interests, and I over his....

I come to say to you and supplicate you, my God, to grant that, by the blood of your Son, he may kiss me with the kiss of his mouth.

What am I without you, O Lord?

What is anything worth if I am not united to you?

And where will I end up if I move away from you even a little?[8]

We make our own the praise in Psalm 103:

Bless the LORD, O my soul,
and all that is within me,
bless his holy name.
Bless the LORD, O my soul,
and do not forget all his benefits—
who forgives all your iniquity,
who heals all your diseases,
who redeems your life from the Pit,
who crowns you with steadfast love and mercy,
who satisfies you with good as long as you live
so that your youth is renewed like the eagle's....

The LORD is merciful and gracious,
slow to anger and abounding in steadfast love.
He will not always accuse,
nor will he keep his anger forever.
He does not deal with us according to our sins,
nor repay us according to our iniquities.
For as the heavens are high above the earth,
so great is his steadfast love toward those who
*   fear him;*

as far as the east is from the west,
so far he removes our transgressions from us.
As a father has compassion for his children,
so the LORD has compassion for those who fear him.
For he knows how we were made; he remembers that
we are dust....

But the steadfast love of the LORD is from everlasting
to everlasting
on those who fear him....
Bless the LORD, O my soul. (Ps 103:1–5, 8–14, 17, 22)

———•◆•———

We entrust to Mary, Mother of Beautiful Love, the resolution we made while we listened to the word and compared ourselves with it.

Part Two

WOMEN IN THE NEW TESTAMENT

Chapter 9

Women in the Genealogy of Jesus

In the New Testament, we find the icon of the family tree of Jesus and take time to revisit our own family tree. We bring to mind the long line of men and women who have transmitted life to us.

Our existence in this world is a grace; it is a miracle. The possibility of life is attained. It is a wonder when life appears, this prodigy given but which is too often discounted or not sufficiently appreciated. Look at nature: how many seeds never become flowers and fruit…how wide the array of possibilities that precede the miracle of life.

We invoke the Holy Spirit to teach us to listen to the love that preceded us so that we will be able to taste the gift of life. May the Spirit help us remember with gratitude those who have transmitted life to us. This gratitude will make space in our memories for praise and blessing.

◯ LISTENING

The genealogy of Jesus according to Matthew offers a significant variation from that of Luke's. Within the rigorous line of masculine generations is inserted the mention of four women. These are women who, for the most part, are foreigners and have irregular marital situations: Tamar (1:3); Rahab (1:5a); Ruth (1:5b); and Bathsheba, the wife of Uriah (1:6b). These women prepare the way for the announcement of the fifth woman, bearer of extraordinary motherhood: the spouse of Joseph, "Mary, of whom Jesus was born, who is called the Messiah" (Mt 1:16).

Let us take a closer look at these forebearers of the Messiah.

The first three women mentioned in the family tree share a common element: they all have origins in pagan populations. According to the Book of Jubilees (41:1), Tamar is an Aramean, Rahab is a Canaanite, and Ruth is a Moabite. Of the fourth woman (Bathsheba), Matthew is strangely silent regarding her name, identifying her only in relation to her first husband, Uriah the Hittite, a foreigner. The mention that Uriah, unjustly eliminated from life and history, is a Hittite, allows the fourth woman to broaden the outlook beyond Israel.

Tamar: the desire of motherhood

The story of Tamar is recounted in Genesis 38. Er, the firstborn of Judah, to whom Tamar is given as wife, "was wicked in the sight of the LORD." Though the reason for this statement is unclear, it must have been very serious, since the sacred author concludes that, because of this wickedness, "the LORD put him to death" (v. 7).

According to Levitical law (see Deut 25:5ff.), Onan, the second son of Judah, was obliged to fulfill a work of charity toward his deceased brother and toward his sister-in-law by taking her in marriage and assuring posterity for his brother. Onan, however, had no passion for life or interest in generating children in his brother's name. He did not intend to assume this responsibility, and he selfishly spilled his semen on the ground. John Calvin comments:

> The Holy Spirit, speaking through the mouth of Moses, condemns above all this impiety: that of Onan, which is, wresting the son from the womb of the mother, flinging it to the ground just as if it had been aborted in violence, revealing himself as cruel, no less than wicked. Besides, in this way he sought to destroy— inasmuch as it depended on him—the human race.[1]

Because of Onan's behavior, the Lord brings about his death also. Judah has one other son, Shelah, but Judah is afraid that Shelah will also die if he marries Tamar. So he decides to send Tamar to her father's house to wait until Shelah has grown up. Time goes by and because Tamar receives no marriage offer from him, she takes the initiative. She disguises herself as a prostitute on the day Judah travels to Timnah for the shearing of his flock. When he sees the disguised Tamar, he has relations with her, unaware that the woman is his daughter-in-law.

When Judah finds out that his daughter-in-law has become pregnant, he does not hesitate to pronounce the sentence: "Bring her out and let her be burned" (Gen 38:24). Tamar then sends to her father-in-law his signet, cord, and staff that she had asked for as a pledge before giving herself over to him. Judah recognizes them and admits: "She is more in the right than I since I did not give her to my son Shelah" (Gen 38:26).

Rahab: courageous mercy

The Book of Joshua (2:1ff.; 6:22–25) speaks of Rahab, the prostitute of Jericho. There is no confirmation in biblical tradition that speaks of Rahab, "the wife of Solomon," of whom Matthew writes. The evangelist was probably reconnecting to a Judaic tradition that is no longer accessible. Nevertheless, it is a fact that in Judaism Rahab is considered just because she acknowledged the God of Israel. She is the first convert. The Letter to the Hebrews commemorates her as a model of faith: "Through faith Rahab the prostitute survived" (11:31); and the Letter of James exalts her faith, which is expressed through works: "Rahab the prostitute [was] also shown to be righteous by her works..." (2:25).

The prostitute of Jericho opens her door to two strangers. Unlike the inhabitants of Jericho, they do not seek her body. Looking them in the eye, Rahab perceives their fear, and she is guided by mercy, offering them food and shelter. In exchange, she asks for mercy, not for herself alone but also for her entire family.

Ruth: steadfast sentiments

An entire book of Scripture is dedicated to Ruth. Her story, interwoven with that of Naomi, is an enthralling account that undoubtedly offers the most beautiful praise of a foreign woman found in the Bible. Ruth is a Moabite widow who is urged by her mother-in-law to return to her own people, to her "mother's house." Yet, unlike her sister-in-law, Orpah, Ruth decides to remain with her mother-in-law, Naomi:

> "Do not press me to leave you or to turn back from
> following you!
> Where you go, I will go; where you lodge, I will
> lodge;
> your people shall be my people and your God my
> God.
> Where you die, I will die—there will I be buried.
> May the LORD do thus and so to me, and more as
> well,
> if even death parts me from you!" (Ruth 1:16–17)

Ruth is a splendid model for us. Like Abraham, she leaves her homeland, her father's house, and her gods. She expresses her deep affection for Naomi in her total reception of Naomi's people and God: "your people shall be my people and your God my God." Like Abraham, Ruth marks a new beginning. Ruth, the Moabite, the gleaner of grain in the fields of Boaz of Bethlehem, is the foremother of David, who decisively marks a new turn in Israel's history.

At Ruth's wedding to Boaz, the authorities and people
of Bethlehem address a joyful salutation to Naomi, saying
that this foreigner will "build up the house of Israel" to the
same degree as Leah, Rachel, and Tamar.

> "May the LORD make the woman who is coming into
> your house like Rachel and Leah, who together built up
> the house of Israel.... [T]hrough the children that the
> LORD will give you by this young woman, may your
> house be like the house of Perez, whom Tamar bore to
> Judah." (Ruth 4:11–12)

Bathsheba: wife of a slain foreigner

The incident of Bathsheba is famously recounted in
Second Samuel 11:1–12, 24. Again, of the four women
included in Jesus' family tree, she is the one whom the
evangelist does not name. He introduces her as the wife of
Uriah, the foreigner who was killed.

We immediately associate two things with Bathsheba:
her extraordinary beauty and the sin of adultery. The
account of Second Samuel shows Bathsheba as rather passive, and the sin of adultery to be David's above all. He
admits this in his *Miserere:* "according to your abundant
mercy blot out my transgressions" (Ps 51:1). Bathsheba is
the beautiful woman the king takes to satisfy his desires:
"David sent messengers to get her" (11:4).

The first and only words the narrator puts in the mouth
of Bathsheba regarding the life she has conceived are "I am
pregnant" (2 Sam 11:5). Tears follow these words—tears

for the death of Uriah, her husband (2 Sam 11:26), and for the death of her baby boy. But God, extraordinarily great in pardon, will choose this woman to give continuity to David's throne. The Lord loved Solomon, the second son of Bathsheba, and sent to him the prophet Nathan, who called him Jedidiah, which means "beloved of Yahweh" (see 2 Sam 12:24–25). That does not diminish the fact that Bathsheba gave the Lord a "helping hand" by convincing David of the advantage of choosing Solomon above all his sons. Bathsheba was a capable woman who knew how to align herself with the right people and how to steal the king's heart (see 1 Kings 1:11–31).

∽ Toward Deeper Listening

What the four women of the genealogy have in common is not sin but the fact of election. They are "vessels of election" by whom God is served, albeit in an unusual way, in order to bring his will to completion. God reserves for himself the path of freedom.

Tamar, Rahab, and Ruth are introduced by divine design into the great promise. These foreign women mentioned by the evangelist Matthew remind us that there is not only Hebrew blood flowing in the veins of Christ. Martin Luther understood this very well when he, in speaking of Tamar, whom he considered to be a Canaanite, commented:

> In the same way Christ shared the blood of the Canaanites and his body shared in the seed of Abraham

and Canaan—this he did in order to declare from the beginning that God does not refuse people: how much more true it is that he receives them with open arms and is so gracious as to take these [body and blood] upon himself. [2]

BIBLICAL TEXTS

God calls the prophet from the womb of his mother:
  Jer 1:5.

God set me apart before I was born and called me:
  Gal 1:15.

Jerusalem is the maternal womb for all people:
  Ps 86 (87).

In Christ those who are far off become near:
  Eph 2:11–22.

DIALOGUE AND COMPARISON

We now go from listening to meditation with the help of some questions. We allow ourselves to be personally summoned by the word, and we compare our life to Jesus Christ, the Word of the living God.

1. We revisit our origins, from the time in our mother's womb, recalling the life transmitted through our parents. When we speak of our ancestors, it can mean that we "visit the dead" within that Communion of Saints, which binds us together, living and deceased, in one embrace. Interiorly we experience gratitude toward them all.

What do I remember about the lives of my parents and grandparents, the quality of their gifts and characteristics?

Do I consider my parents or my grandparents as "gifts of God" even when they are old and infirm, and if their powers of reasoning are diminishing?

I ask to be reconciled, if needed, with my mother, my father, my grandparents.

2. The foreign women of the family tree of Jesus remind us of the wealth of dialogue and cultural exchange linked to the interweaving of races and different cultures. Above all, they attest to the universal openness of the divine election; prefiguring in a certain sense the Church coming forth from the Gentiles, from non-Hebrew origins. They represent our ethnic roots and the fact that we have been grafted "into a cultivated olive tree" (see Rom 11:16–24).

What does this mean for my own experience of faith?

How do I relate with my Jewish brothers and sisters and with believers of other religious faiths?

3. To recall our own origins is to remember our "received identity." Above all else, life is a gift. No one chooses his or her own parents, family, or homeland. On this foundation, we base the journey of our personal growth, of acquired identity. We are not our mothers or their fears, our fathers or their convictions. We are the fruit of their love along with the interplay of our own freedom.

In calling to mind the gift of life I have received, do I experience a sense of wonder and gratitude?

How do I live the gift of freedom?

☙ Prayer

We contemplate the icon of Elizabeth and Anna.

Luke does not mention any women in the genealogy of Jesus (see Lk 3:23–38). However, in chapters one and two he presents two outstanding figures who act as the hinge between the Old and the New Testaments: Elizabeth and Anna. These women are both advanced in years. One has a husband but no children; the other became a widow at a young age and has lived in the Temple in prayer and works of charity since her husband's death. In a certain sense, we can consider them our spiritual grandmothers.

Grandchildren usually get along with their grandmothers. Sometimes a grandmother has more time to listen to us than a mother does. Grandmothers also have a longer life-experience to recount and share. As our grandmothers, Elizabeth and Anna remind us that life unfolds over time; great things do not happen spontaneously—and neither do faith and hope.

Elizabeth and Anna remind us of the poor ones of the Lord, those whose hope is entirely founded on the Lord and whom the Bible presents as the heirs of salvation. When God, in extreme condescension, becomes a man, the poor and humble acknowledge and welcome him. Jesus is immediately recognized by the humble Elizabeth and by the prophet Anna. Symbolically, these two women inaugurate a new age, the era of the Messiah. They appear beside Mary, the Mother of Jesus.

We pray the text of Luke 1:41–45. We pause over the jubilation of John in the womb of his mother and Elizabeth's joy when Mary's greeting reaches her: "But how is it that the mother of my Lord should come to me?"

We contemplate Anna, the aged prophet awaiting the Messiah. We ask for the same enthusiasm she had in speaking to everyone about Jesus (see Lk 2:38).

———•◆•———

We entrust to Mary, humble mother of the Lord, the resolution we made while we listened to the word and compared ourselves with it.

Chapter 10

Mary: Woman of the Yes and Mother of the Magnificat

Messianic times commence with the yes of Mary, the virgin mother of the Lord. In her, the seal of the promise that forged the long chain of hope reaches its fullness:

> But when the fullness of time had come, God sent forth His Son, born of a woman, born under the Torah, so we could be adopted as God's sons. (Gal 4:4)

We dedicate this stage of our journey to Mary's call and her ready response that is a model for ours:

> She stands out among the poor and humble of the Lord, who confidently hope for and receive salvation from Him. With her the exalted Daughter of Sion, and after a long expectation of the promise, the times are fulfilled and the new Economy established, when the Son of God took a human nature from her, that He might in the mysteries of His flesh free man from sin.[3]

Pieter Van Der Meer, a well-known Catholic writer in Holland, speaks of God as the great poet of the universe. The Greek meaning of the term "poet" refers to those whose actions make a new reality spring forth. God is the poet who has no limitations, who calls all things into being, according to that beautiful biblical expression: he called the light and "it obeyed him, trembling; the stars shone in their watches, and were glad; he called them, and they said, 'Here we are!'" (Bar 3:33-34).

Mary's call is part of this awesome poetry of God, who has dreams and plans of salvation for humanity. God takes the initiative. He calls. He enters into Mary's life in an unforeseen manner, calling her to go along with his plan. And Mary entrusts herself fully to the Lord's request. Just as the light and stars, Abraham, Moses, and the prophets, Mary promptly responds with her "here I am." She is that feminine servant of the Lord, "Behold, the handmaid of the Lord" (Lk 1:38).

The Holy Spirit gifts us with the memory of our own vocation and renews in us the joy of this call and the willingness to mature fully and unconditionally in the way the Lord desires us to today.

LISTENING

Hail, full of grace

The Gospel of Luke sets the scene of the annunciation in Nazareth of Galilee. Mary seems to be in her home because the angel Gabriel, sent by God, "came into her presence" (Lk 1:28). Iconography and art have made familiar to us the image of the annunciation with Mary at prayer. Some paintings depict her holding the Book of Psalms. She is not portrayed, we realize, during an official time of prayer at the synagogue, but at home, in an attitude of listening and communion with the Lord that permeated her daily life.

Hail, full of grace, the Lord is with you! Rather than calling her by name, Gabriel calls Mary "full of grace," as if Mary is receiving a new name, a new identity. The term *cháris*, "grace," indicates the merciful and benevolent love of the Lord who gives salvation. Mary is "full" of God's favor, of his love; and she fully corresponds to and welcomes it.

Gabriel's greeting evokes the joyous announcement of the prophet Zephaniah regarding Jerusalem:

> Sing aloud, O daughter Zion; shout, O Israel!
> Rejoice and exult with all your heart, O daughter
>   Jerusalem! ...
> The king of Israel, the LORD, is in your midst....
> The LORD, your God, is in your midst, a warrior who
>   gives victory;
> he will rejoice over you with gladness, he will renew
>   you in his love;
> he will exult over you with loud singing as on a day of
>   festival. (Zeph 3:14–18)

"Nothing is impossible for God"

To the humble girl of Nazareth is announced maternity through the work of the Holy Spirit: the child to be born of her will be "Son of the Most High." The prophet Nathan had announced to David the continuation of his reign through a descendent, profoundly bound to God: "I will be a father to him, and he shall be a son to me" (2 Sam 7:14). Now Gabriel announces the fulfillment of that oracle. The throne of David, "established forever," will be given to that Son of the Most High who will be born of Mary. In him everyone "born of a woman" (Gal 4:4) will become a child of God, the Most High.

"How will this come about?" asks Mary. She is engaged to Joseph, a man of the house of David, but they have had no sexual relationship—nor do they intend to. Mary's affirmation "I do not know man" implies an intentional, deliberate life-project. Not only does she not know man, she has no intention to know man, that is, to have a sexual relationship. This possibility should not surprise us. At the time of the New Testament, the celibate life was practiced, for example, by the men of the Essene community at Qumran. One might object that there were no analogous feminine situations in which celibacy was lived. Every Hebrew woman desired to be if not the mother of the Messiah, at least one of his ancestors. However, in this regard, the Bible tells the significant story of one extraordinarily important woman, the story of Judith, whose name means "Judea." Young and beautiful, this splendid Hebrew woman was left a childless widow very shortly after her marriage and was not interested in a new marriage. She refused the various proposals offered, and chose to live totally for God and the good of her people (see her story previously recounted in this book). This means that it was *not* unthinkable that a woman could choose to live celibately. One can then presume that Mary *also* had deliberately chosen to live a virginal life, as affirmed in the perspective of John Paul II.[4]

Within this narrative, Mary's question functions to move the story forward, and that happens with the angel's reassuring response: "The Holy Spirit will come upon you, and the power of the Most High will overshadow you..." (Lk 1:35).

More than an explanation, these words challenge our faith, which is urged on by a new "sign": Mary's sterile and elderly cousin Elizabeth, like Sarah before her, awaits a son. Mary is called to remember that "nothing is impossible to God." This is the foundation upon which rested Abraham's faith that Sarah would bear a son (see Gen 18:14).

Behold, the handmaid of the Lord

Mary's response to the angel's words is an unconditional yes. Hers is not a "yes, but"—she simply says "yes." She places all her trust in the Lord, as her cousin Elizabeth acknowledges: "Blessed is she who believed that there would be a fulfillment of what was spoken to her by the Lord" (Lk 1:45).

Behold. Mary does not limit herself to offer something, she offers herself. Within that *behold*, she gives all of her freedom and her very self. She who is "full of grace" offers this open and generous response to the Lord.

Behold. Mary wants one thing: whatever pleases the Lord. She considers herself God's servant and so presents herself as such in the Magnificat: "He had regard for the lowliness of his handmaid," a servant (Lk 1:48). The figure of the servant of Yahweh outlined by the prophets (particularly Deutero-Isaiah) and fulfilled in Christ, is, for the first time, reflected in a feminine person.

> Sacrifice and offering You did not desire,
> but You have prepared a body for me;
> Burnt offerings and sin offerings gave You no pleasure.
> Then I said, "Behold, I have come to do Your will,
>   O God,"
> as it is written about me in the scroll of the book.
> (Heb 10:5–7)

In perfect harmony with the Messiah's sentiments, Mary lives according to the same quality of faith and obedience.

The song of Mary

Mary breaks into the song of the Magnificat in the house of Zechariah (see Lk 1:40), traditionally thought to have been located in Ain Karem, in the mountains of Judah, about 112 miles from Nazareth and about six miles from Jerusalem.

Above all, the hymn is linked to what has happened in Zachariah's house. Here are two women, one sterile and the other a virgin, both graced by the Spirit of the Lord. For both women, prayer is their whole way of being, of living, and of self-expression.

Like Sarah, Elizabeth is unexpectedly liberated from the humiliation of sterility. She experiences the flowering of life, a life that moves and leaps. At Mary's greeting the baby jumps within her womb and she is "filled with the Holy Spirit" (as is John, see Lk 1:15). Elizabeth cries out loudly, as in liturgical acclamations, and she prophesies, blessing the "mother of my Lord." In faith, Elizabeth welcomes the Lord as "my Lord."

Elizabeth's blessing serves as the first fruits of a hymn through which all generations will proclaim blessed the humble servant of the Lord.

Mary echoes her cousin's words, although she directs her praise away from herself and to the Lord. Her praise leads back to its source. Mary's joy expresses in an eminent way the exultation of messianic times, the experience of the fullness of salvation, the praise of the "great things" (Greek *megála*) worked by the Powerful One for her and for all those who fear him.

Mary raises her heart and canticle to the Lord from whom all things descend. It rises toward the Lord who deigns to look on her, in her poverty, renewing the marvels of the Exodus. We seek to listen profoundly to this canticle in order to savor the poetic beauty, the play of contrasts, and the power of actions. We try to listen to the Magnificat in a new way, distancing ourselves from our familiarity and habitual mode of reciting it, which have become mechanical and formal.

There are two parts or strophes of the Magnificat to highlight:

— the first strophe, which is in the singular (vv. 46–50);
— the second, which is in the plural (vv. 51–55).

In the first part, the focus is definitely on Mary—Elizabeth, the house, the husband, the neighbors, all seem absent. At center stage is Mary, the mother-servant of the Lord, reaching out to him with all of her being.

The second part fills, enlarges, and almost widens to the infinite: every generation is involved—a multitude of the poor and the small, humble people. Mary's canticle is their song. They sing and dance as the people once did on the shores of the Red Sea.

There are thirteen verses in the Magnificat, and, with the exception of the first two, Yahweh is the subject. The Lord is magnified and exalted; he gives final judgment over history and overturns social positions. The praise that opens and sets the tone describes the Lord's holy Name and work in the story of salvation. It is a celebration, in litany form, of God's intervention in history, a sevenfold account (the number seven is a symbol of fullness) of salvific actions:

- he has shown might with his arm;
- he has scattered the arrogant;
- he has pulled down the mighty;
- he has exalted the lowly;
- he has filled the hungry with good things;
- he has sent away the rich;
- he has helped Israel.

The first expression, "he has shown might with his arm," clearly evokes the Exodus, when Yahweh manifested

his power against Pharaoh's arrogant oppression of the
Hebrew people. Moreover, God shows his might for the
sake of Israel, the object of God's affectionate mercy, which
he helps in fidelity to his promise to Abraham.

The horizon is clearly set out before us. On the shore of
the Red Sea the prophet Miriam, the sister of Moses, sings
praise to the Lord's victory:

> "Sing to the LORD for he has triumphed gloriously;
> horse and rider he has thrown into the sea." (Ex 15:21)

On the summit of the New Testament, Mary of Nazareth echoes this sentiment:

> "My soul gives praise to the Lord...
> For the Mighty One has done great things for me...
> He has shown might with His arm,
> scattered the arrogant...
> He has pulled down the mighty... and exalted the
>   lowly...." (Lk 1:46–52)

Who are the powerful and rich against whom the Lord
flexes his arm, that is, his power? The words do not seem
to take aim at the powerful because they are the constitut-
ed authority or the rich because they are rich. Rather the
powerful and the rich are seen as the historical embodi-
ment of the arrogant mentioned in the verse. The arrogant
assume God's place and claim to govern the world according to their brand of justice, without any fear of the Holy
One. They do and undo according to their own pleasure
and based on their advantage. They are not concerned with
the poor, the widowed, or the orphan. They do not concern

themselves with securing justice but with securing their own "throne."

They are the pharaohs of their times, thinking only of possessing complete command, imagining they can even win heaven with their riches and power. But they delude themselves, and they have already determined their destiny, like the selfish rich man in Jesus' parable (see Lk 16:19–31). In it the poor man Lazarus sits beside Abraham on a throne of glory while the rich man (nameless because it is not worth remembering) is cast into the midst of torments. God takes the part of the oppressed against the oppressor; he takes the part of those who fear him, who are poor and wretched, against the pleasure-seekers consumed by selfishness.

As God once freed Israel from Egypt, the Lord's mighty arm will deliver the poor of the earth from misery. His work of liberation will overcome the obstacles of the world's powerful who, like Pharaoh, often sit on thrones of violence and oppression. Thus the canticle of Mary, like the ancient biblical hymns it evokes, is a powerful burst of messianic hope.

ᢙ Toward Deeper Listening

In Mary, the humble handmaid of the Lord, we contemplate our ecclesial vocation and the perfect response to that vocation. Virginity and motherhood "were united in her in an exceptional manner, in such a way that one did not exclude the other but wonderfully complemented it."[5]

The Church is also both virgin and mother. According to Saint Clement of Alexandria, the Church

> is virgin and mother, integral and inviolate as a virgin, loving as a mother; she calls her children to herself and nourishes them with holy milk, which is the Logos made a child.[6]

Saint Augustine confirms:

> The Church is virgin, therefore she gives birth. She imitates Mary who gives birth to the Lord. Like her, the Church also gives birth and is virgin.... You to whom I speak, you are members of Christ. Who has given you birth? I hear the voice of your heart: Mother Church! This holy mother, honored, like Mary, gives birth and is virgin.[7]

Saint Bede also asserts that "Each day the Church gives birth to the Church."[8]

The call to evangelization is a call to motherhood. The First Letter of Peter sees a strict relationship between the rebirth generated through the word announced and the mission of evangelization, which can be considered a life-giving action:

> You have been born anew, not from perishable seed but from imperishable seed, through the living, abiding word of God.... This word is what was proclaimed to you in the good news. (1 Pet 1:23–25)

Regenerated by the word, we are invited to "proclaim His saving deeds, who called you out of darkness into his marvelous light" (1 Pet 2:9).

In her encounter with her cousin Elizabeth, Mary sings of the wonders fulfilled in her by the Almighty. To evangelize is to magnify God for the great works accomplished in us by his mercy. Evangelization is not simply instructing others, but also sharing with them an experience of salvation. It is to sing our Magnificat.

⬭ BIBLICAL TEXTS

Born of a woman in the fullness of time: Gal 4:4–7.
Our call in Christ Jesus: Eph 1:3–14.
Ecclesial maternity/paternity: 1 Cor 4:15.

⬭ DIALOGUE AND COMPARISON

We now go from listening to meditation with the help of some questions. We allow ourselves to be personally summoned by the word, and we compare our life to Jesus Christ, the Word of the living God.

1. We are receivers of the divine proclamation, chosen by God and freely called. We are asked to "give birth to the Son of God" and to give him to others as Mary did.

Am I aware of this call?

How do I live my specific Christian vocation?

How do I witness to the hope within me to the people I encounter during the day?

2. The Second Vatican Council presents Mary as the one who "stands out among the poor and humble of the

Lord, who confidently hope for and receive salvation from him."[9] We compare our attitudes with those of Mary: with her faith, humility, total availability to the divine will, and active listening to the word.

Can I discover Mary's attitudes in myself? To what degree?

Which of Mary's attitudes do I need to strengthen in my journey of faith?

Do I trust in God as Mary did?

∽ PRAYER

Let us contemplate the icon of the Magnificat, looking at Mary who rises and sets out on a journey to Elizabeth's house. She resembles the ark of the covenant, aware of the presence of her God (see Ex 40:35).

We contemplate the meeting of two women who have believed in the word.

We make Mary's song our own.

To believe is to acknowledge God who is present and active in history. It is to recognize him as the faithful one who has also done great things for us.

The Magnificat discloses the "not yet" of hope.

Though Mary sings: "he has pulled down the mighty from their thrones, and exalted the lowly," there is a king on the Jewish throne: Herod. This man instills fear in the people and proves his terrible violence when he orders the slaughter of the infant sons of Bethlehem and its surroundings (see Mt 2:16). He is like Pharaoh in his deeds. But the words of the canticle are not merely a poetic allusion. In the light of the resurrection, Mary's Magnificat proclaims fulfillment. In Jesus, the Poor One raised up, the promise of glory is unveiled for the humble of the earth.

The story of salvation is consistent: God has already made known his preferences and his criteria for judgment. Therefore, believers can extol, "he has pulled down the mighty from their thrones," even if that hour has not arrived for them.

The Church sings the Magnificat in the liturgy of Vespers at the hour when day and night meet, as if to say that the obscurity of darkness must contend with Mary's canticle in which she bears witness to the light, because the Lord's mercy is forever.

———•◆•———

We prolong our prayer of thanksgiving, and to Mary, woman of the yes, we entrust ourselves and the resolution we made while we listened to the word and compared ourselves to it.

We sing the Magnificat.

Chapter 11

Women Healed by Jesus: Faith that Invokes Salvation

Jesus met many women on his journeys, and many benefited from his healing powers on the physical, psychological, moral, and spiritual levels. In Luke's Gospel, we encounter the symbolic number of seven women for whom Jesus worked miracles of healing and raising from the dead. Only one is known by name: Mary Magdalene, "from whom seven demons had gone out" (Lk 8:2). The others are introduced by their social and relational status: mother-in-law, widow, daughter, and so on. Others remain anonymous.

Does it suffice merely to be ill or psychically and spiritually disturbed to be healed by Jesus? Are there conditions for this healing or some criteria to follow? The Gospels, particularly Luke's, which we will follow in this *lectio divina*, give a lot of space to this theme. They clearly point out that healings, as God's gift, are always somehow also an option—a personal choice bound to faith, risk, and love.

We invoke the Spirit of Jesus, our Savior, who gives us the awareness of our own infirmities, healing our ailments and reinvigorating our lives.

⌒ LISTENING

Continuing with the Gospel of Luke, we allow ourselves to be taken up into the account of three healings, or, more precisely, the story of three women marked by suffering and humiliation who experience saving love in Jesus' restorative power.

Simon Peter's mother-in-law: healing to free for service

Among the first of Jesus' healings was one on behalf of a woman, Simon Peter's mother-in-law. The synoptic Gospels agree on this.

It is the Sabbath and Jesus spends the morning in the synagogue. His teaching deeply impresses those present because of the unusual style and authority with which he speaks. His teaching is confirmed by remarkable healings, and the first of these is the liberation of man possessed by a demon. The healing takes place in the synagogue and serves to show Jesus' messianic power: he commands demons with authority and power (see Lk 4:33–36).

"When he left the synagogue he went into Simon's house" (Lk 4:38). In chapter 4 of Luke, we find the first mention of Simon, who has not yet been called (see Lk 5:4–11). Luke does not specify that the house Jesus enters belongs to "Peter"—the reader assumes the evangelist means him. For the first time Jesus enters the house that will become his home in Capernaum. He is there to dine and rest, but he encounters hardship.

> Now Simon's mother-in-law was suffering from a high fever, and they appealed to him on her account. And when he stood over her he rebuked the fever and it left her; she got up immediately and began to serve them. (Lk 4:38–39)

Luke emphasizes the gravity of the woman's fever and another detail that he has much at heart: prayer. Unlike Mark who notes the intervention of her relatives ("at once they told Jesus about her," Mk 1:30), Luke stresses the dimension of prayer that characterizes the members of the household: "they appealed … on her account" (4:38).

And Jesus grants their prayer. He approaches the bed and bends over the sick woman to heal her with the power of his word. He addresses himself more to the fever than to the woman, as if it were a living thing, a demon. Jesus reprimands and threatens it, and the fever immediately obeys him and vanishes. The woman is now free of the infirmity that kept her in bed. She can get up by herself and give proof of her cure by placing herself at the service of her family and guest.

The symbolic value of this healing is obvious. Like the man in the synagogue, Jesus restores the woman to full health and, even more, to her vocation. She is back on her feet and once again able to resume her duties as woman of the house on the Sabbath.

Freed from this strange fever, Simon Peter's mother-in-law recovers the joy of generous and gratuitous service for her family and her new guest and benefactor. That she promptly gets up "to serve them"—prohibited by the rabbis who forbid women to "serve at table"—is already "an indication of new tasks that await the woman in the Christian community."[10]

The hemorrhaging woman: the "touch" that saves

Two miracles are interwoven in Luke 8:41–45: the healing of a woman who has suffered the loss of blood for twelve years (Lk 8: 43–48) and the raising of Jairus' daughter. The latter is inseparably linked to her father, the only person in the Bible with the name Jairus, which in Hebrew means "God shines." Through Jesus, God actually does shine for this grieving father, a high-profile individual who has some social authority as "ruler of the synagogue." His only daughter of twelve years is dying. In his sorrow, Jairus throws himself at Jesus' feet as a slave before his master, and he begs Jesus to go to his house. He gives no thought to his reputation; the only thing that matters to him is his daughter's life. Jesus accepts to go and heal her.

But on the way there, a spontaneous cure takes place:

> Now as Jesus slowly made his way the crowd kept pressing in on him. A woman was there who had had a heavy flow of blood for twelve years. She ... couldn't be cured by anyone. She came up and touched the tassel of his

cloak from behind, and immediately the flow of blood
stopped. (Lk 8:42–44)

This miracle is also found in Mark, who presents the situation a bit more harshly: in vain has the woman spent all
of her savings in consulting doctors. She is now reduced to
misery. Perhaps Luke, whom tradition presents as a doctor,
omits this detail to spare those of his profession from insult.
He limits himself to saying that she "couldn't be cured by
anyone." This suffices to describe the painful reality of the
poor woman. Humiliated by her condition, which has also
rendered her "impure" (see Lev 15:19–27), the woman
hopes to obtain healing while passing unobserved.

She is content to merely touch the "tassel of his cloak."
Luke alone refers to this particularly expressive detail. Is
this need to "touch" even the hem of Jesus' mantle faith or
superstition? True, in comparison with the centurion of
Capernaum who wants to spare the Master[11] the distur-
bance and inconvenience of entering a pagan home and is
convinced that just a word would help his own servant, this
woman demonstrates that her faith is inseparable from the
senses, from what she can touch. Perhaps Jairus is on the
same level. He is bringing the Master to his house so Jesus
can place his hands on his little daughter.

In faith, the woman believes her contact with Jesus'
clothes can heal her. Then the miracle is accomplished.
The woman immediately senses that she is healed—and at
the same time found out. Jesus does not intend to keep this
act hidden; he wants to make it public. "Who was it that
touched me?" he asks as the crowd presses in on him. Peter

is amazed that Jesus even asks such a question. He points out: "Master, the crowd is pressing in on you and crowding around" (Lk 8:45). The people have a perfect excuse, but Jesus insists: "Someone touched me—I could feel power going out from me" (Lk 8:46).

When the woman realizes she cannot hide, she falls trembling before him and, in the presence of all the people, she tells why she touched him and how she had been immediately cured.

The "someone" who touched Jesus had a feminine touch. Unlike the crowd, she touched the Lord not only physically, but with great faith. Jesus turns toward her with tenderness, calling her "daughter" (Greek *thigáter*). Now there is a profound affective bond between them—she is not one woman among many, she is a daughter! Jesus, on his way to heal Jairus' only daughter, has met and healed another daughter. Two daughters: one who has been *losing life* for twelve years (in Semitic culture blood is strictly connected with life) and the other a girl of twelve years whom Jesus goes to in order to call her back to life.

The woman stands before Jesus and he reassures her:

> "Daughter … your faith has saved you; go in peace!"
> (Lk 8:48)

The stooped woman: mercy that unbinds

The third healing story in Luke 13:10–17 is set on the Sabbath. Like his first healing in Capernaum, this healing takes place inside the synagogue (Lk 4:33–36). However, in this case it is a woman enslaved by the evil, his prisoner for eighteen years. This woman is terribly "bent over." (Lk 13:11)

Specialists refer to her probable physical ailment as postural scoliosis. This woman suffers from a curving of the back that is so severe her movements are spasmodic, "she was bent over double and unable to straighten herself up fully" (Lk 13:11).

She has suffered patiently for eighteen years (the symbolic number for fullness: three times six). Despite her pain, she is in the synagogue on the Sabbath, as was perhaps habitual for her. Consequently, we see she has kept faith and confidence in the Lord of life.

No one introduces her to the Master; neither does the poor woman come forward to ask for prayer. She is simply there, stooped. In that position, she cannot even see Jesus, but for her Jesus has eyes as well as voice and hands. Let us take note the unfolding of the text:

> When Jesus *saw her*
> he *called out* to her
> and *said*,
> "Woman,
> you have been set free from your illness!"
> Then *he laid his hands on her*.

Jesus sees and has compassion on this woman, suffering and hunchbacked, compassion for her deformed body. He sees her and calls her to himself. She is a woman ground down and crushed under a burden too heavy to bear. She is an image of the people: "My people are bent on turning away from me. To the Most High they call, but he does not raise them up at all" (Hos 11:7).

Jesus wants to unbind her, to free her.

> "Come to me, all you grown weary and burdened, and I will refresh you. Take my yoke upon you and learn from me, for I am gentle and humble hearted, and you will find rest for your souls; for my yoke is easy and my burden light." (Mt 11:28–30)

Under Jesus' healing touch, the woman stands erect, as befits a human being. She can finally look up to heaven and glorify God.

Yet someone laments that cure. The synagogue's leader speaks with the people who have come to be healed on the Sabbath. It is too unpleasant to attack Jesus directly (after all, it could prove disagreeable to make an enemy of the healer); it is better to rage against the people: "There are six days on which it is proper to perform work, so come be healed on those days and not on the Sabbath" (Lk 13:14).

How outrageous to place the glory of God and the life of man and woman in opposition. Jesus, the benevolent healer, reveals that the glory of God—as Saint Irenaeus said well—is the human person fully alive. Perhaps that poor woman would have continued to praise God without giving much thought to the synagogue leader's indignation, but Jesus defends her and all the oppressed:

> "You hypocrites! Does not each of you untie your ox or donkey from the manger and lead it off to water on

the Sabbath? Was not it proper for this daughter of Abraham, whom Satan had bound for all these eighteen years, to be released from this bond on the Sabbath day?" (Lk 13:15–16; see also Lk 6:6–10)

The woman was "bound"; Satan had her tethered, indeed subjugated by the heavy yoke that deformed her body. Now this "daughter of Abraham" (in the Old Testament only men were referred to as descendants of Abraham, as "sons of Abraham") is free; Jesus has released her from her burden, even if it is the Sabbath day, so that she might glorify God, as is fitting at all times and above all on the Sabbath.

⌘ Toward Deeper Listening

Jesus reveals in the most vibrant way God's pathos for suffering humanity. He fulfills the meaning of his name: "Savior."

The fundamental characteristic of healing signs is undoubtedly the gratuitousness of the divine initiative. However, this does not stop us from underscoring the human conditions that make healing possible: salvation is an option, a free choice of man and woman. In this sense, one can walk with faith, humility, and love.

The sequence of the stories of healing we have presented permits us to understand three very different situations:

◆ In the case of Simon Peter's mother-in-law, members of the family are concerned with the woman's well-being and request the healing of Jesus.

◆ In the second case, the sick woman takes the initiative. Though suffering from an incurable and humiliating illness, the hemorrhaging woman takes a risk, venturing through the mob of people until she achieves her purpose: to at least touch the tassel of Jesus' cloak.

◆ In the third case, the poor woman seems surrounded by emptiness; she asks for nothing and no one intercedes on her behalf. Her situation recalls the paralytic at the pool of Bethesda who has no one to help him into the pool when the water is stirred up (see Jn 5:1–9). However, just the woman's being there in the synagogue is a living cry that reaches Christ and moves him to compassion. (See the cry that goes up to God from his oppressed people, Ex 3:7–9.)

Saint Irenaeus writes:

> [T]he glory of God gives life; therefore those who see God receive life. And because of this, he who is unintelligible, incomprehensible, and invisible made himself visible, comprehensible, and intelligible to men, in order to give life to those who comprehend and see him [through faith]. For this reason the Word was made dispenser of the grace of the Father in order to benefit men, so that those for whom he had ordered all "the economy" of salvation, showing God to men and presenting man to God.
>
> He has rendered God visible to men with many providential interventions, so that man would not be completely deprived of God and fall into his own

nothingness, because the glory of God is man fully alive and the life of man is the vision of God.[12]

∽ BIBLICAL TEXTS

Called to share in serving as Christ serves:
  Lk 22:24–30.

God does not delight in the death of the living:
  Wis 1:13–15.

Come to me, all you whose burdens are too heavy:
  Mt 11:28–30.

∽ DIALOGUE AND COMPARISON

We now go from listening to meditation with the help of some questions. We allow ourselves to be personally summoned by the word, and we compare our life to Jesus Christ, the Word of the living God.

1. In Simon Peter's house, symbolic of the Church, the family's manner of relating to Jesus surpasses the level of simple information. Their words are a humble and heartfelt intercession: the family prays for healing.

How do I allow for this type of sensitivity toward others in my life?

Do I limit myself to speaking about another person's sufferings, or do I make them my own and humbly ask for the Lord's healing?

2. Health is not only a personal good; one asks for good health in order to serve others. It is possible for selfishness

to be the hidden motive behind requests for healing—spiritual or physical. The apostle Paul asked the Lord three times to free him from a particular suffering, and he received this response: "My grace is enough for you, for my power is made perfect in your weakness" (2 Cor 12:9).

Do my requests for healing truly express the desire to serve?

How do I see the gift of health? Do I recognize that in every condition I am called to fully accomplish God's will, to complete the mission the Lord has entrusted to me?

3. The hemorrhaging woman believed that to be healed it was enough to touch the tassel of Jesus' mantle. We are given the grace not only to touch his cloak but also to experience him in the sacraments of the Church. Yet it is not enough for us to touch or even to eat. One must "touch with faith."

How do I celebrate the sacraments of Eucharist and Penance? Do I value them as opportunities for personal and communitarian healing?

4. Rather than a response to an explicit request, at times we experience healing as a gift offered freely by divine love. God's free gift was offered to the woman stooped for eighteen years. However, it is significant that even in this condition the woman was found in the synagogue.

Do I confidently await the hour of salvation?

How do I help my family and community to persevere in prayer, especially in times of protracted physical and spiritual illness?

Do I turn to Jesus to find peace and relief when I feel tired and bent under the heavy burden of misunderstandings or difficulties at home or at work?

∞ Prayer

We allow ourselves to be helped in our prayer by the icon of the Canaanite woman who requests Jesus' healing not for herself but for her daughter (see Mt 15:21–28; Mk 7:24–30).

Because of her humility and courageous insistence, this woman gets Jesus to work a healing beyond the confines of Israel, overcoming discrimination between Jews and pagans. We imagine an abundant feast, a banquet where there is enough bread for children and dogs. This woman's faith is so great that she does not need "to touch" (not even the tassel of Jesus' cloak). She believes that even a crumb of bread from Jesus is enough to nourish everyone: "These all look to you to give them their food in due season … you open your hand, they are filled with good things" (Ps 104:27–28).

Such faith surprises Jesus: "O woman, great is your faith! Let it be done for you as you wish!" (Mt 15:28) That mother's faith is so strong that the Savior does not need to "enter into her house." As in the case of the centurion of Capernaum, Jesus can work for her a cure at a distance.

We offer to the Lord our requests for healing. We give thanks to God for his mercy, praying Psalm 100:

Make a joyful noise to the LORD, all the earth.
Worship the LORD with gladness;
come into his presence with singing.

Know that the LORD is God.
It is he that made us, and we are his;
we are his people, and the sheep of his pasture.

Enter his gates with thanksgiving,
and his courts with praise.
Give thanks to him, bless his name.

For the LORD is good;
His steadfast love endures forever,
and his faithfulness to all generations.

———•◆•———

We entrust to Mary, mother of mercy, our resolution and the word we will practice in our lives with her help.

Chapter 12

The Samaritan Woman: The Memory of a Wedding

John the evangelist presents Jesus' dialogue with the Samaritan woman within the framework of a wider section that opens and closes at Cana of Galilee (Jn 2:1—4:54), where we have the first revelation of Jesus. This section is characterized by "signs" and "dialogues" and by the faith-response of his disciples, who at Cana "believed in him" (2:11); Nicodemus, who represents Judaism (Jn 3); the Samaritan woman and her people (Jn 4:4–42); and finally the royal official, who represents the faith of the pagans: "he believed, along with his whole household" (Jn 4:53).

We rest at the well of Sychar. We want to meet Jesus just as the Samaritan did. With her, we want to allow ourselves to be led by him toward the truth, toward a fuller understanding of him and ourselves.

The evangelist John sets the encounter between Jesus and the Samaritan woman at the well of Sychar. Typically in

Scripture when a stranger and a woman meet at a well, the story ends with a wedding. We read in the Book of Genesis how Abraham sends his servant to his homeland to find a wife for his son Isaac. He meets a splendid young woman, Rebecca, at a well (24:10–51). Jacob meets his greatest love, the beautiful Rachel (29:9–14), at a well. Moses also encounters his future bride at a well (Ex 2:15–22). Why then, knowing what this scene could evoke, would John set the encounter of Jesus and the Samaritan woman at a well? This question will guide us in listening to the text.

We invoke the Spirit of Christ, the living water, who gives us the ability to adore "in spirit and in truth" as the Father desires from his sons and daughters in messianic times, the time of the wedding feast.

ෆ LISTENING

Jesus is returning from Jerusalem to Galilee. Rather than taking the road that runs along the shore of the Mediterranean or returning by way of the Jordan, he chooses the most arduous route, through the mountains of Samaria. He arrives at the gates of Sychar about midday. His disciples go to the city to buy something to eat. Jesus, tired from the journey, sits near the well traditionally associated with the patriarch Jacob.

At the well of Sychar

A woman comes to the well to draw water. Why has she chosen to draw water at the hottest time of day? Generally, at that hour people stay indoors to eat and rest. We know that women usually went to draw water in the evening (see Gen 24:11), at the end of the day when they could take a moment to relax and chat with friends. The well, the center of small villages as the main water source, is also a place for socializing.

Therefore, why has this woman come to the well at such an unusual hour? Perhaps in the simple hope of *not* meeting other women, so she can get her water quickly and return home undisturbed. Her story must have been known in the city and was probably the object of jokes and gossip when the women gathered at the well.

So there she is at the well—and there is a stranger, a man. She says nothing. He puts forth a request: "Give me a drink" (Jn 4:7). Subtly and artfully, the evangelist John begins one of the most beautiful dialogues of the Gospel. Jesus takes the initiative; it is he who "provokes" a conversation with the woman. At one point, however, she takes charge and directs the conversation. In the end, she interrogates Jesus. To this woman, and to her alone, Jesus expressly declares himself to be the Messiah.

If you knew the gift of God!

From the outset the woman keeps her distance. The stranger's request goes against social norms: "How is it that you, a Jew, ask me, a Samaritan woman, for a drink?" (Jn 4:9). The evangelist notes the bad blood that existed between Jews and Samaritans for reasons both political and religious. The Samaritans had constructed a temple on Mount Gerezim and claimed it a legitimate place of worship. The Jews considered the Samaritans half-pagan idolaters. So the woman marvels that a Jew would address a word to her and, what's more, request something of her.

How does Jesus answer her question? He does not offer socio-political explanations, but raises further suspicion. Just as she has defined him as a Jew, he casts her idea into doubt: "If you knew the gift of God and who it is who's saying to you, 'Give me a drink,'" (4:10). She really does not know who he is. She does not know the gift of God who stands before her.

The woman listens curiously: gift of God, living water —how odd is this stranger's way of reasoning. It is entirely impractical:

> "Lord, you have no bucket and the well is deep, so where do you get the living water from? Surely you are not greater than our father Jacob…?" (4:11)

Jesus offers no explanation. He continues with his enigmatic language: "Everyone who drinks this water will thirst again. But whoever drinks the water I will give him will never thirst.…" The woman responds immediately: "Lord, give me this water so I won't become thirsty…" (Jn 4:13–15). Jesus has hit the mark!

Go call your husband

Now there is a turn in the dialogue. The Master puts forth a new request: "Go call your husband and come here."

Poor woman! She had gone out at noon to spare herself smirks, comments, and inferences, and here this stranger brings up the critical point. "I don't have a husband," she responds swiftly. He returns: "You were right … you have had five men and the one you have now is not your husband" (Jn 4:18). Notice she is not offended. Rather, Jesus' knowledge of her life opens her eyes to his mysterious identity: "Lord, I see that you are a prophet" (Jn 4:19).

It might seem that the woman is cleverly trying to change the subject, but she is not trying to start a theological discussion to avoid the reality of her own life. Jesus has shown that he has an intimate knowledge of her story that only God or a man of God, such as a prophet, could have. The woman acknowledges Jesus as a prophet. In this role, he has much more to reveal to her.

From her truth to his truth

We can gather that the narrative functions in this way because of the text that follows. Jesus does not reproach the woman for trying to change the subject, for evading his request. Instead, he answers to the point, moving to a less enigmatic and more explicit revelation:

> "Believe me, woman, the hour is coming when you will worship the Father neither on this mountain nor in Jerusalem… God is spirit and those who worship Him must worship in spirit and truth." (Jn 4:21–24)

The woman replies: "I know that the Messiah is coming…."

Now Jesus reveals his true identity: "I who am speaking to you am he" (Jn 4:25–26).

The scene comes to life. The disciples return and marvel to find Jesus speaking with a woman, though they hold themselves back from asking questions. For her part, the Samaritan woman breaks away. She even leaves without her bucket of water. She has tasted the living water that Jesus promised, and she has no time to lose. She possesses news so beautiful that she must share it. She runs into the city, and she feels like a free woman.

No longer must she conceal her story. She does not fear scornful looks and ironic smiles. She enthusiastically recounts her experience. Only yesterday that story was motive for humiliation and shame. Today she can speak of it freely. Even more, her life becomes the basis of her own witness and announcement: "Come see a man who told me everything I've done! Could this be the Messiah?" (Jn 4:29).

∽ TOWARD DEEPER LISTENING

The biblical encounters at a well offer the same plot or narrative scheme:

- A man travels to a strange land (Abraham's servant, Jacob, Moses, and Jesus in Samaria, a foreign territory in a certain sense).
- The man finds a well.
- A woman (or more than one woman as in Ex 2:16) arrives to draw water.

  ◆ A conversation ensues regarding the water drawn.

  ◆ A conversation follows regarding the man's identity.

  ◆ The woman runs home to give the news about the man.

  ◆ The stranger is invited to the house. A dinner and wedding follow.

Naturally, each story has its own variations, and in our case the variation on the theme is at the end: there is no wedding.

How are we to interpret this surprise ending? On the historical level, the answer goes without saying: Jesus was not married. But on the symbolic level? Why would the evangelist John place the setting at a well knowing that his readers would expect a particular ending?

It seems as if John likes playing with double meanings, for example when he speaks of living water. The Samaritan woman would have thought of living water as a spring of running water. But on the lips of Jesus "living water" recalls the Spirit. Here, playing on the narrative theme of a meeting at a well, John has another surprise for us, a variation on the wedding theme at the beginning of the story. The woman who goes to the well is not like Rebecca, Rachel, or the daughters of Reuel. She is not looking for a husband— she has had five! Her problem is distinguishing her true husband. This woman represents her people, the Samaritans, whom the Jews considered heretical and unfaithful. They had abandoned the God of Israel, the "true and only husband."

Saint Augustine saw in the Samaritan woman a figure of the Church that would arise from the Gentiles:

> [L]et us recognize ourselves in her, and in her we give thanks to God for ourselves. She was the figure, not the reality; for she both first showed forth the figure and became the reality. For she believed in him, in fact, who placed the figure before us. "Come then to draw water." She had simply come to draw water as men and women do....
>
> Since the woman carried with her a pitcher with which to draw water, she marveled that a Jew would ask her for a drink, something that the Jews never do. However, he who was asking her for a drink was thirsting for the faith of the Samaritan woman....
>
> He asks her for a drink and then promises to quench her thirst. He is needful as one who waits to receive, and he abounds as one who is able to satisfy. "If you knew," he says, "the gift of God." The gift of God is the Holy Spirit. But Jesus speaks to the woman in a manner still veiled, and little by little a way to her heart is opened. Perhaps already he teaches her. What is in fact sweeter and more affectionate than this exhortation? "If you knew the gift of God and who it is who is saying to you, 'Give me a drink,' you would have asked him and he would have given you living water."
>
> Therefore, what water will he give to her, if not that of which it is written: "For with you is the fountain of delights" (Ps 36:9)? In fact, how can they have thirst who "feast on the abundance of your house" (Ps 36:8)?[13]

∽ Biblical Texts

> "They have forsaken me, the fountain of living water":
> Jer 2:13.
>
> "With joy you will draw water from the wells of salvation": Isa 12:1–6.
>
> "My soul thirsts for … the living God": Ps 42:2–3.

∽ Dialogue and Comparison

We now go from listening to meditation with the help of some questions. We allow ourselves to be personally summoned by the word, and we compare our life to Jesus Christ, the Word of the living God.

1. Seated beside the well, Jesus awaits us. He also promises us the living water that gushes forth into life eternal.

"If you knew the gift of God…" Do I truly know this gift of God? Do I live of and for him?

2. Jesus, the Messiah, calls us to live the truth of our life.

Where is my heart? Is God the only true Lord for me? Does God give full meaning to my loves: fiancé or spouse, children, friends? Or is my love for God one among the many?

3. The Samaritan woman felt known in her deepest truth—known, not judged. Known and loved.

Do not be afraid to continue speaking with Jesus. The water that he promises washes and gives rebirth.

∞ PRAYER

We rest at the well of Sychar.

In our contemplation, we pause over the various elements that make up the icon of the Samaritan woman:

- ◆ The well that Jacob gave to Joseph.
- ◆ Jesus who was tired and sat at the well at the sixth hour.
- ◆ The woman who comes to draw water.
- ◆ The key passages of the dialogue.
- ◆ The disciples' entrance on the scene.
- ◆ The bucket left behind by the Samaritan woman, and disciples offering food to Jesus.
- ◆ The golden fields, ready for harvest.
- ◆ The success of the mission among the Samaritans.

Allowing ourselves be guided by the Spirit, we share in prayer what resonates within us regarding this icon. We pray:

Make us sensitive to your thirst, Lord Jesus!
May your words, "give me to drink,"
continue to fill us with wonder.
The woman of Samaria did not understand initially.
She marveled how you, a Jew,
would ask her for something to drink.
Even less is it understood by those who,
having seen you hang on the cross, mock your thirst....
They want to see if Elijah will come to take you down,
and at the end they raise to your lips

a sponge dampened with vinegar.
Your thirst, Lord, is not quenched by the water of Sychar
nor is your hunger satisfied with the food
bought by the disciples.
You hunger to accomplish the work of he who sent you,
of he who so loved the world as to give his only Son.
You thirst and hunger for our salvation.
You, our God, seat yourself at the well
and wait for a sip of water from those
who sense you could die from burning thirst.
You, fountain of living water, teach us to find you again
in the well of our hearts...
The Truth lives within us.
Lord Jesus, help us to live our life in truth,
teach us to adore the Father in Spirit and in truth.
Make us like the enamored bride,
who invokes you united to the Spirit:

"The Spirit and the Bride say, 'Come!'
And let whoever hears say, 'Come!'
Come, whoever is thirsty,
whoever wants to receive the gift of living water!"
(Rev 22:17)

———•◆•———

We entrust to Mary, the faithful spouse of the new covenant, our resolution and the word we will practice in our lives with her help.

Chapter 13

Women Following Jesus: Free for the Gospel

The Gospels say little about the women disciples of Jesus. It seems they are recalled only when it cannot be avoided, when theirs is the only witness to the supreme events of the Master's death and resurrection. In effect, the first two evangelists remain silent concerning the women disciples except during Jesus' passion and death. Obviously, they were disciples before those events; they did not just turn up for the first time beneath the cross.

Fortunately, Luke records that women were also present from the beginning of Jesus' ministry. Not only men steadfastly followed the prophet of Nazareth. Contrary to the custom of the time, Jesus accepted women among his followers (see Lk 8:1–3). He deemed them able to listen to and announce the word of God. He challenged the dominant culture not only with regard to women who were considered sinners, but also, and even more, because he included women in his work of evangelization.

In his missionary travels at the side of the apostle Paul, Luke must have repeatedly experienced the welcome and generous availability of many Christian women. He must have encountered intelligent, generous, and capable women who opened their homes to itinerant missionaries. Women were passionate collaborators with them for the sake of the Gospel, as the story of Lydia suggests (see Acts 16:14–15). The Spirit decisively opens new horizons for man and woman.

We invoke the Spirit of the only Master so we may be witnesses to and heralds of the Gospel.

☞ LISTENING

Itinerant Disciples

The news that a group of women is traveling with Jesus is given in the context of a "summary" that informs us of his evangelization activity:

> It happened next that he went traveling through city and village, preaching and proclaiming the good news of the Kingdom of God, and the Twelve were with him as well as some women who had been healed from evil spirits and illnesses—Mary who was called the Magdalen, from whom seven demons had gone out, and Joanna, the wife of Chuza, Herod's steward, and Susanna, and many others who provided for them out of their possessions. (Lk 8:1–3)

The mention of the presence of women in Jesus' itinerant group constitutes an absolute novelty in the culture of the time, particularly in the environs of Palestine (recall how his own disciples "were amazed that he was speaking to a woman" Jn 4:27). This highlights that women not only have a peripheral role in the group, but also are involved at the very heart of Jesus' activity: the announcement of the Gospel.

Jesus evangelizes Israel systematically; today we would say that his disciples took to the streets: "he went around the surrounding villages teaching" (Mk 6:6). Everyone must have the possibility of hearing the good news and of being converted.

Jesus does not go alone. With him are the Twelve and the women. The Twelve represent the entire People of God: on one hand, they are the sign that Jesus addresses himself to all of Israel (the twelve tribes). On the other hand, they indicate that Israel has believed and accepted Jesus' call to conversion. This Israel *in nucleus*, gathered around Jesus, is sent to evangelize the entire populace. Jesus is therefore the fulcrum of an intense evangelization effort, which becomes even more organized with the sending of the seventy-two disciples (see Lk 10:1; cf. Ex 24:9).

What position and role do the women have in this fervent activity? Like the Twelve, these women *follow* Jesus in every sense of the word: physically, walking in his footsteps, and spiritually, sharing his plans. When Jesus preaches, they are near him; they *listen* to him. Further, when walking with him they *see* what he does and how he conducts himself.

Luke 8:1–3 informs us that these women have had personal experience of the healing power of Jesus: they "had been healed from evil spirits and illness" (Lk 8:2). Perhaps for this reason they served (*diekónoun*) Jesus and his followers "out of their possessions" (Lk 8:3). The grace these women received has made them capable of loving in deed, able to offer *diakónia* to answer the various needs of an itinerant group. Three of these women are mentioned by name: Mary who was called the Magdalene; Joanna, the wife of Chuza; and Susanna.

Mary Magdalene

Mary Magdalene is mentioned first, a primacy acknowledged by all four evangelists for her proclamation of the resurrection. Undoubtedly, she had to have been a woman of great prominence in the early Church.

One of the Jesus' first followers, Mary Magdalene has "seven demons" cast out from her. Hers is a particularly grave case of possession, as is explicitly cited in Luke 11:26. Is it possible to give a name to the "seven demons"? Is it fair to interpret them in terms of sexual transgressions and, consequently, to see Mary Magdalene as the sinner (prostitute) spoken of in Luke 7:37–50? In themselves, sin and diabolical possession are not synonymous in the New Testament. Yet already in the ancient Church, we find an overlap between the story of the pardoned prostitute, whom Luke does not name, and the story of Mary Magdalene from whom "seven demons" were expelled. The seven demons may be read as equaling all the devilry expressed in sex, or the demon of *porneía*.

Here then is the traditional image of the Magdalene as a former prostitute who lets down her long hair so she can dry the tears she has shed over Jesus' feet.[14] Luke 8:2 does not agree with this superimposition of texts. Instead, Luke's Gospel offers a relevant angle regarding the psychological identity of Mary Magdalene: she is undoubtedly a woman restored to herself, given back her freedom through the exodus of seven demons. Therefore, this woman now lives her freedom as a service of love. For this reason she is a model of Christian freedom expressed in service (see Gal 5:1–15).

Joanna and Susanna

The second woman mentioned in Luke 8:3 is Joanna. There is no hint of her in the other Gospels. Luke instead speaks of her again in 24:10, and in that instance places her second to Mary Magdalene.

Luke reports Joanna's civil and social status: she is the wife of Chuza, an administrator for Herod. Therefore, she comes from an elevated social situation. The question then arises: if she is married, how can she roam about with Jesus? Luke does not explain, and this complicates our understanding and opens up various hypotheses. Is Joanna a widow? If that is the case, why does Luke, who particularly admired Christian widows, not say this?

> If Chuza was still alive and occupied an important post at Herod's court, the situation is even more complicated. Would he have agreed with his wife making a decision that would put his career in jeopardy? Or would

Joanna, besides abandoning her position, have had to bear her husband's hostility and loss of affection? There is no mention of possible children of the marriage, so there is no point in further speculation on this point, on which there is no evidence. [15]

What could have motivated Joanna to follow Jesus? Because Luke does not explicitly say, we can suppose that what was said of the other women applies also to her: the experience of healing and of redemptive love.

The third woman mentioned by Luke 8:3 is Susanna, of whom nothing else is known. But her name is already enough to allow us to conclude that with Jesus there was a group of women, and that some in the community still remember their names. These women had the courage to live the austere life necessary in following Jesus in his tireless wanderings.

From Galilee to Jerusalem

Now we imagine ourselves beneath the cross. Jesus has already given over his spirit into the Father's hands (see Lk 23:46). The crowd has returned to the city beating their breasts in sorrow, but there is a small group of followers who show no signs of leaving. They are Jesus' friends and faithful companions from Galilee, easily identifiable by their speech (we recall what happened to Peter on the night he betrayed Jesus). Luke mentions these companions three times: in referring to Jesus' death, burial, and resurrection (see Lk 23:49; 55–56; 24:1–11).

Besides being present beneath the cross, these women are also the first to draw near the sepulcher, in this way confirming his death. Their witness crowns Easter morning when the angels help them to remember the words of Jesus: "Remember—he spoke to you *(hymin)* when he was still in Galilee.... Then they remembered..." (Lk 24:6–8).

In a certain sense, memory is identified with the heart, the place where words are kept and cared for. With the resurrection, the memory of Jesus' words springs into consciousness. The first to "remember" are these women. The two angels remind them of the words spoken to them by the Master "when he was still in Galilee."

The Gospels do not mention Jesus explicitly revealing his death and resurrection to the women. Perhaps there was no need. At the beginning of chapter 8, Luke has already informed his readers that the group traveling with Jesus contained some women. Therefore the reader quickly understands that what Jesus says (such as the announcement of the passion) as they travel would have been heard by the women. They know as much as the Twelve. It was only a question of "remembering." It is precisely what happens at the tomb the morning after the Sabbath. The two men-angels help the women of Galilee revive "the memory" of Jesus' words. It is a memory that revives faith.

∞ Toward Deeper Listening

Luke's attention to the women is continued in the Acts of the Apostles. The Pentecost experience portrays the unity of the Christian community, represented by the Apostles "with some women and Mary the mother of Jesus and his brothers" (Acts 1:14). This ideal composition of the original nucleus highlights the spiritual continuity between Jesus' time and that of the Church. The outpouring of the Spirit is revealed as overcoming every barrier of sex, race, and culture.

This is the same interpretation that Peter makes of the prophecy of Joel 3:1–5 in his first discourse:

> "I will pour out My Spirit on all flesh,
> and your sons and your daughters will prophesy,
> Your young men will see visions,
> and your old men will dream dreams;
> Yes, upon my servants and handmaids will I
> Pour out My Spirit in those days,
> and they will prophesy." (Acts 2:17–18)

The gift of prophecy characterizes the entire community; sons and daughters now are all empowered to announce the good news.

Paul expresses praise for the missionary dedication of his collaborators, among whom are women. One thinks of Priscilla (also referred to as Prisca), the wife of Aquila. Paul encounters this couple at Corinth and benefits from their hospitality for about a year and a half (see Acts 18:1–11). In the final greetings of his letter to the Romans, Paul remembers them with profound gratitude (notice Prisca's name precedes her husband's, which is unusual and seems to confirm this woman's position of prominence):

> Greet Prisca and Aquila, my co-workers in Christ Jesus. They risked their own necks to save my life, and not only I but also the Gentile churches thank them. Also greet the church at their house. (Rom 16:3–5)

The list of persons greeted opens with the name of Phoebe, deaconess of the church of Cenchreae (see Rom 16:1). The apostle further greets Mary, who has worked much for the community of Rome; the couple Andronicus and Junias, "my kinsmen and fellow prisoners"; Tryphaena and Tryphosa "laborers in the Lord"; the beloved Persis, "who has worked so hard for the Lord"; the mother of Rufus; and also Patrobas and Julia. The list of collaborators continues with the sister of Nereus, Olympas, and all the saints who are with them (see Rom 16:6–15).

This list of collaborators is impressive. Behind these names are faces and characters and, above all, love and toil. From the start, evangelizing is an activity in which women collaborate on the front lines, with total commitment.

⬭ Biblical Texts

Revisit the prophetic vocations of Miriam:
  Ex 15:20–21; Deborah: Judg 5:4; and of Huldah:
  2 Kings 22:14–20.

Discipleship yields brothers and sisters of Jesus: see
  Mt 12:46–50; Mk 3:31–35; Lk 8:19–21.

Paul affirms the end of every discrimination between
  man and woman: Gal 3:28.

∞ DIALOGUE AND COMPARISON

We now go from listening to meditation with the help of some questions. We allow ourselves to be personally summoned by the word, and we compare our life to Jesus Christ, the Word of the living God.

1. In its essentials, Christian life is expressed in following Christ, "for you to follow in his footsteps" (1 Pet 2:21). The women of the Gospels, first among them Mary of Magdala, traveled the path of Jesus from Galilee to Jerusalem. They listened to his word, observed how he conducted himself, and allowed themselves to be molded by his way of life.

How do I live the following of Jesus Christ?

Do I compare myself daily with his word?

Do I allow myself to be educated by Jesus' sentiments, his prayer, his dedication to the reign of God?

Am I his witness in every aspect of my life?

2. The following of Jesus is lived by the women of Galilee in the manner of *diakónia*, generous service.

How do I live *diakónia* in the Church and in society?

Do I feel honored to be able to put at the service of the Gospel and of the ecclesial and civil community the various gifts that the Lord has given me (health, time, intelligence, education, skills, intuitions, and so forth)? Or am I excessively careful to guard myself, my health, my time, my wealth?

3. Paul reveals his capacity for friendship and affection toward his men and women collaborators. He shows his

gratitude and appreciation for the devotion to the Gospel and the various forms of *diakónia* demonstrated by the women.

What kind of relationship do I have with other pastoral workers?

Do I know how to listen to the ideas of others?

Do I appreciate their work?

Do I communicate my point of view and my insights with fairness and humility?

Do I acknowledge my own failures and mistakes?

⟿ PRAYER

We contemplate the icon of the new family of Jesus (see Mt 12:46–50; Mk 3:31–35; Lk 8:19–21).

Among the women and men disciples of Jesus there is a bond of "kinship" brought to birth by the word of God. The common adherence to the will of the Father creates "family," new brotherhood and sisterhood.

Discipleship is accomplished as a community of those who listen to the word of God and put it into practice. Jesus refers to this new, vital relationship, based on the efficacious fruitfulness of the word, when he responds to the woman who exclaimed: "Blessed is the womb that bore you, and the breasts that you nursed at!" He says: "Blessed are those who hear the word of God and keep it!" (Lk 11:27–28).

We want to thank the Lord Jesus for this blessedness and for having made us his family, his brothers and sisters:

Thank you, Jesus,
for having called us to be with you,
for having called us to follow you
in your loving obedience to the Father's plan.
Thank you for the honor you give us
in associating us with your mission
of evangelization and salvation.
Help us not to draw back.
Lord Jesus, do not permit us,
after having followed you,
to retreat into our little problems and concerns.
Free us from living for ourselves.
Help us to remain open to listen to your word
and to be receptive to the challenges of our era,
capable of discerning your will in the signs of the times,
in the questions, often unexpressed,
of the people to whom you send us.
Teach us to speak with the Father
and to speak of his love to our brothers and sisters.
Awaken in us the gift of your Spirit
so that we will allow ourselves to be
completely guided by him
in our life and mission.

———•◆•———

We entrust to Mary, Mother and Disciple of the Lord,
our resolution and the word we will practice in our lives
with her help.

Chapter 14

Martha, Mary, and Lydia: Their Hospitality and Homes

In his itinerant preaching, Jesus found hospitality in the home of two sisters, Martha and Mary (see Lk 10:38–42).

John the evangelist informs us that they lived in Bethany, a village on the eastern ridge of Mount Olivet, close to Jerusalem. In their house, Jesus feels at home, among friends. He is with them six days before his Passover. Martha serves at table and, on that occasion, Mary covers his feet with perfumed and precious oil, raising murmurs among the guests.

The woman makes the home. What Jesus experiences at Bethany in Martha's home, Peter experiences in Jerusalem at the home of Mary, and Paul at Philippi in the home of Lydia. In the early Church, great importance was given to the gift of a welcoming home. Entering as a guest in Martha's house, Jesus leaves behind a fundamental message: only "one thing is necessary." What is needed is not anxious *diakónia*, but welcoming love, a love that listens.

We invoke the Spirit of the Lord so that he will help us make our house and our Church places of hospitable welcome, where the Lord can continue to be the Master, and where women, no less than men, learn to sit at his feet and listen.

The house of Martha

During the fatiguing work of their mission (the "course of their journey," Lk 10:38), Jesus and his disciples find generous hospitality from Martha and Mary. In the Bible, a guest is always the bearer of a message. The question is what message Jesus will bring when he enters Martha's home.

Martha is presented first; she is probably the older sister. The house is "hers" and Mary is then introduced as "her" sister.

The two sisters relate to Jesus in very different ways. Martha gives him a fitting welcome by offering many services. Mary prefers to remain at his feet and to listen to him. Because of this, their characters have often been set against each another: Martha as the symbol of the active life, Mary of the contemplative life. Some suggest that behind the contrast between the two sisters is a conflict present in the early community, between activists and ascetics. With this background, one might ask what is more important at the heart of the Christian community: service or *diakónia* (Martha), or listening to the word of Jesus (Mary)? Perhaps the more radical question is how we must welcome the Lord. There are two methods of welcome: Jesus prefers Mary's method. We will see why.

∞ LISTENING

Martha feels so honored to welcome the Master to her home that she hardly knows what to do for him. She would like everything to be perfect; she would like to offer him the finest hospitality. Perhaps she also is a bit emotional—when one is expecting an illustrious guest, emotions can take over. After the initial welcome, heartfelt and expressive, there is a noticeable change, as if the situation has gotten out of hand. Jesus is no longer the center of attention. Obviously Martha is working for Jesus, she gives of herself to serve him, but she gets so carried away she looses sight of the object of her service: Jesus.

That evening Martha must have been particularly tense. Perhaps she is behind schedule; her reputation is at stake. She asks why Mary does not give her a hand. Since the Master arrived, Mary has been there at his feet, lost in listening to him. Is it possible that she has not noticed how much her help is needed? Not even Jesus seems to realize how much Martha needs Mary's help.

Martha decides to interrupt. Under the pressure of her anxiety, she intervenes in an inappropriate manner. Rather than turning to her sister, she takes her complaint directly to the Master:

> "Lord, doesn't it matter to you that my sister has left me to serve alone? Tell her to give me a hand!" (Lk 10:40)

Her tone is more like that of a landlady. What happened to the welcoming and generous woman of the house?

What has provoked this sudden change of attitude? There seems to be an explosion of bitterness in Martha's words. Perhaps it is because she feels left alone in serving. Martha expects Mary to see what she needs. Focused on her expectations, she does not communicate with her sister; she does not have the simplicity to say, "Please help me, Mary." She expects Mary to understand, and she expects the Lord to intervene and give her justice.

Perhaps there is something more. Martha feels offended by her sister's attitude. Her being at the feet of Jesus breaks the fixed norms of Judaic culture of the time. "To be at the feet of" someone is a symbolic expression. In biblical language, it means to be someone's disciple. Paul spoke of his having grown up "at the feet of Gamaliel," one of the most famous of rabbis. However, women were not permitted to be at the feet of a rabbi to learn how to interpret Scripture. Houses of study *(bet hammidrash)* were open only to men. From this perspective, perhaps Martha was asking Jesus to help her sister to return to within the parameters of the traditional role of women: "Tell her to give me a hand!"

Jesus, however, is uneasy with this request. He turns to the woman of the house with affection, but at the same time firmness, calling her by name twice: "Martha, Martha." This is exactly how he responds to Simon Peter when he is in imminent danger of great temptation (see Lk 22:31). In fact, Martha is being tempted to value herself only insofar as she renders a function of services. "You're anxious and upset over many things." (Lk 10:41) In contrast, Mary, the younger sister, recognizes the visitation of the Lord (cf. Lk 19:44). She suspends her activities and rejoices in his presence: "Blessed be the Lord ... he has visited and set his people free" (Lk 1:68). Her apparent non-doing, seated at the feet of Jesus like his disciples, coincides with the choice of the "better part." And this will not be taken away because Jesus does not intend to deprive her of the right to be at his feet as an authentic disciple.

Martha's house is not limited to being a house of rest. By the very fact of the Master's presence, it may now function in the role of school, of a house of study, with the novelty that women are not excluded. In the house of Martha, whoever desires to, man or woman, can remain as a disciple at Jesus' feet.

The house of Mary, mother of Mark

In his second volume, the Acts of the Apostles, Luke presents other homes and welcoming women. In Jerusalem, Peter, after being imprisoned by Herod, miraculously escapes. Yet, half dazed, he is unable to give an account of how it all came about.

> And when he realized this he went to the house of Mary, the mother of John who is called Mark, where a considerable number of people were gathered in prayer. When he knocked at the entrance door, a young maid named Rhoda answered it, and when she recognized Peter's voice, out of joy she did not open the entrance

but ran in and announced that Peter was standing at the entrance. "You are crazy!" they told her, but she insisted that it was so. Then they said, "It's his angel!" But Peter kept knocking, and when they opened the door and saw him they were astounded. He motioned to them with his hand to be silent and then told them how the Lord had led him out of the prison and said, "Tell this to James and the brothers!" Then he went out and left for another place. (Acts 12:12–17)

This house must have been familiar to Peter if, when he found himself in such a situation, he instinctively went there. The fact that he finds the community gathered there in prayer means that Mary, the mother of Mark, has opened her home to welcome the community. It is a place where they could gather and pray. Just as in Martha's house, here one experiences the Lord's presence.

In the moment of testing and persecution, the brothers and sisters of Jerusalem spontaneously gather in this house to share their concern for Peter's life and together to invoke the Lord: "the Church was offering fervent prayers to God on his behalf" (Acts 12:5). Mary's house is the icon of a community that believes in the risen Lord and in his powerful intercession. It is a community that gathers and prays in the name of Jesus. God listens to the prayer that comes forth from Mary's house and sends his angel to free Peter.

We hope that our homes may also become houses of Mary, places of welcome, of simple and fraternal hospitality, and of prayer.

The house of Lydia

We place ourselves within the context of the Pauline mission. Amid the difficult experience of itinerancy, behold a house that is generously open to welcome the evangelizers. Luke, the only evangelist to recount how Jesus had found hospitality in the house of Martha during his itinerate preaching, presents another woman, Lydia. She puts her house at the disposition of the missionaries and the community being formed by their preaching.

> We set sail for Troas and made a straight run to Samothrace, reached Neapolis the next day, and from there went to Philippi, which is a Roman colony and the leading city in that district of Macedonia. We stayed several days in that city. On the Sabbath we went outside the gates to the river, where we thought there would be a place of prayer, and sat down to talk with the women who had gathered there. There was a woman named Lydia listening there—a dealer in purple cloth from the city of Thyatira and a worshipper of God—and the Lord opened her heart to heed the words Paul was speaking. After she and her household were baptized she offered this invitation, "If you consider that I am a believer in the Lord, come and stay in my house." And she prevailed upon us. (Acts 16:11–15)

Let us pause a moment to delve into this story.

The initial information regarding the trip to Troas and Philippi (verses 11–12b) helps us to remember the position of the itinerant missionary and the difficulties involved.

Paul and his missionary companions are devoid of security and human support, entrusting themselves solely to the word of the Lord. There is no mention of where they lodge when they arrive in Philippi for the first time. They spend the days preceding the Sabbath looking for the places where Jews gather to pray. According to Acts, Paul's mission begins in the synagogue. However, in Philippi there was no synagogue. Sabbath prayer is held beside the river, because water is needed for the ablutions. On the morning of the Sabbath, our missionaries set out from the city gate heading toward the nearby Gangites River.

It is interesting to note that at Sabbath prayer we find (chiefly or only?) some women. Men are not mentioned at all. One could presume that this is an open-air oratory where those sympathetic to Judaism, the circle of the so-called *God fearers*, come to pray on the Sabbath. Paul and his followers minister to these women who are close to the Jewish faith. The attention immediately centers on one of them: Lydia, the first "European Christian."

Lydia of Thyatira is from a city renowned for its industry in purple dye (see Rev 1:11; 2:18–29). She is a dealer in purple goods, a business that has made her wealthy and independent. In effect, Lydia reveals herself as a gifted woman who is particularly sensitive to Paul's preaching. Luke, however, is concerned to clarify that the initiative of her conversion comes from on high: "the Lord opened her heart to heed the words Paul was speaking" (Acts 16:14).

The grace of God opens Lydia's heart and she surrenders, entrusting herself totally, without any resistance.

After her conversion, she and her entire family are baptized. Lydia's home then becomes the mission base for Philippi. Her invitation is obligatory: "she prevailed upon us" (Acts 16:15). This expression evidently highlights the woman's generous hospitality. She reciprocates, so to speak, the grace of faith with the gift of her assets. The Lord Jesus has found room in this woman's life. She promptly adheres to him in faith and immediately opens the doors of her home to the preachers of the word: "If you consider that I'm a believer in the Lord, come and stay in my house" (Acts 16:15).

Lydia opens her home completely. She has now discovered something much more valuable than purple dye! This treasure is not to be kept to herself, but it is one she feels she must propose to others with her characteristic enthusiasm. She is so convincing that she leads her family to faith. In Lydia's house is born the first domestic church of Philippi.

∞ Toward Deeper Listening

There seems to be a continuity in Luke's works: Martha's house that offers welcome to Jesus and his group; Mary's house where Peter gathers together with the community; and Lydia's house where Paul finds hospitality.

In the early Church, committed to itinerant evangelization, these houses where the missionaries received lodging were a sign of the Lord's provident care, like a womb of the nascent Church. Within them took place the listening to the word, the celebration of the Lord's Supper, and the experience of *koinonía*, communion.

How do we reread these experiences in the light of our own times? What challenges do they offer? When Jesus and his word truly enter a house, the doors open without fail. This is true whether on a personal, parish, or community level.

⌒ Biblical Texts

> The widow of Zarephath welcomes the prophet Elijah: 1 Kings 17:9–16.
>
> The woman of Shunem generously welcomes the prophet Elisha: 2 Kings 4:8–17.
>
> "Wherever you enter a house, stay there…": Mk 6:10; cf. Mt 10:11–14; Lk 10:5–9.

⌒ Dialogue and Comparison

We now go from listening to meditation with the help of some questions. We allow ourselves to be personally summoned by the word, and we compare our life to Jesus Christ, the Word of the living God.

1. With particular strength, the early Church experiences the Lord's salvific action within the home, where the reality of the domestic church is born. Our contemporaries also demonstrate sensitivity to the family dimension of community, to small communities that allow for greater understanding and communication. Various ecclesial groups and

movements have returned to valuing the importance of the home in the light of evangelization and catechesis. Parishes are challenged to adopt a more familiar face not only with regard to offices and organization, but also in order to be a home in the community.

Is my home a place of welcoming, fraternity, and evangelization? Do I open my home to friends only or to the poor, the immigrants, and the needy?

What do I think about the pastoral reality of Mary's house, where Peter finds the community united in prayer? What about Lydia's house, where Paul and the other missionaries announce the word?

2. After her generous welcome, Martha becomes so carried away with the tasks at hand that she risks losing sight of the Lord for whom she performs her service. She experiences bitterness and anger and does not realize how she is caught up in herself. This can happen to us when we lose sight of the One for whom we serve others.

How do I welcome others? Am I attentive to the person or do I focus on making a good impression? Do I radiate Mary's serenity or Martha's agitation?

3. The Master is present and thus Martha's home is not only a house of rest, it is also a school, a house of study and prayer, where anyone who desires to can sit at the feet of Jesus as his disciple.

How open am I to listening to the Master? Do I know how to stay at his feet in order to learn wisdom permeated by prayer and grateful welcome?

PRAYER

We contemplate the icon of the house of Martha, where Jesus sits as Master and teaches us not to separate contemplation and service, which by their nature are profoundly united. John Paul II writes:

> Meditation on God's word, and on the mysteries of Christ in particular, gives rise to fervor in contemplation and the ardor of apostolic activity. Both in contemplative and active religious life it has always been men and women of prayer, those who truly interpret and put into practice the will of God, who do great works. From familiarity with God's word they draw the light needed for that individual and communal discernment which helps them to seek the ways of the Lord in the signs of the times.[16]

We bring to prayer the behavior of Martha and Mary.

We ask pardon for the times when we, like Martha, under the burden of many obligations, have neglected to be attentive to the Lord in the person of the brother or sister who asks us to listen to and welcome him or her.

We thank the Lord for the frequent possibilities we have to hear his word and for the various helps he gives us in order to understand the word better.

Together we pray:

O Lord Jesus,
help us to live in your presence
in every moment of our day,
in every situation of our life.

Grant that we may welcome you
with the generous affability of Martha
each time you present yourself at our home:
be it as an itinerant evangelizer,
as a poor person, or someone traveler.
Grant that we may not allow ourselves
to be absorbed by the things that need to get done,
but that we will manage to maintain order
in our priorities
and above all a sense of service.
Give us wisdom of heart
that allows us to be spiritually at your feet, like Mary,
even when we are burdened with many activities.
Give us, Lord, the strength to collaborate
in the building up of a Church
that has a more familiar face,
where each person feels at home,
among brothers and sisters.
Grant that our communities will accomplish
that spiritual and material koinonía
that existed in Lydia's house.

————•◆•————

We entrust to Mary of Nazareth, the mother of welcome, the resolution we made while we listened to the word and compared ourselves with it.

Chapter 15

Two Women Named Mary:
Feminine Icons of the Paschal Mystery

Jesus travels to Jerusalem, every pilgrim's desired goal and the place where he will complete his earthly life. At the sight of the city, Jesus weeps—it has not understood the way of peace nor comprehended the visitation of the Lord (see Lk 19:28–44). On Jesus' way of the cross the "daughters of Jerusalem" (Lk 23:27–31) will tearfully accompany him. The women are the last to take leave of his tomb and the first to return to it.

Three women, all named Mary, remain particularly close to Jesus: Mary, his mother, who will follow him to the foot of the cross; Mary of Bethany, who seems to have a presentiment of his death and lavishes on him the most expensive of ointments; and Mary Magdalene, who early in the morning on the day after the Sabbath is already at the tomb. These women clearly articulate the three great moments of the paschal mystery: the beginning of the passion, the death, and the resurrection.

In this encounter we pause over the passages regarding Mary of Bethany (Jn 12:1–8) and Mary Magdalene (Jn 20:1–18), two splendid images of the Church in love with her Lord.

We invoke the Spirit whom Jesus has unleashed from the heights of his cross so that we might be rendered capable of a passionate love that is stronger than death.

◌ Listening

At Bethany: a love that gives everything

In Jerusalem there is already a plot to murder Jesus. Only two days are left till the Passover, and Jesus expresses to his disciples the gravity of the moment: "You know that the Passover will be in two days, and the Son of Man will be handed over to be crucified" (Mt 26:2). While his enemies determine the when and the how, he retires to the home of his friends in Bethany.

The first two Gospels mention a certain "Simon the leper." Instead, the evangelist John places us in the home of Martha. Here a dinner is offered for Jesus and also to celebrate the presence of Lazarus, the friend Jesus had raised from the dead. Martha serves at table while Mary, the woman Luke has portrayed at the feet of Jesus completely absorbed in his words, surprises everyone with an extraordinary gesture:

> So Mary took a pound of very expensive pure oil of nard and anointed Jesus' feet and wiped his feet dry

with her hair, and the house was filled with the fragrance of the oil. (Jn 12:3)

Immediately Judas protests the waste, and from his point of view he is right. That perfume could have been sold for "three hundred denarii"—ten times the price he had received to "give over" the Master! Judas is described as an antithesis of Mary of Bethany. If she represents agapic love, he is the opposite.

Jesus defends Mary. She has recognized the Poor One and has done for him what was in her power to do: "Let her be; let her keep it for the day of my burial, for the poor you always have with you, but me you do not always have" (Jn 12:7–8).

Nearing his passion, Jesus encounters two women who are alike and who, in different ways, express the same logic: the poor widow who throws her last two coins into the Temple treasury, and Mary of Bethany. It doesn't matter whether the gift is two coins or 300 denarii. The women share the fact that they have given everything. The widow's two coins of insignificant value certainly causes no one to accuse her of waste; no one even notices. However, she casts her whole being into the treasury of God. It is the same case with Mary's perfumed oil. She could have poured just enough to honor the guest and give a festive touch to the house. She would have spared herself the criticism of those scandalized by such waste.

Both of these women seem a little irrational or at least lacking in common sense. In the logic of welcome, even the most generous, demands that if you have very expensive perfumed oil, you use it sparingly, as with any precious thing. What gets the guests talking is not the gesture but the evident exaggeration, the waste. Jesus, instead, appreciates and understands what is behind the gesture—the waste speaks of love's measure. The one who loves reasons with the heart and spares nothing. So the logic of love is not knowing how to measure, but knowing how to give everything.

Woman, why are you crying? Who are you looking for?

Mary Magdalene is crying. She had gotten up while it was still dark on that morning of the first day after the Sabbath (see Jn 20:1). She wanted to be at the tomb as early as possible to honor the body of her beloved Master with aromatic spices. When she arrives at the tomb, the stone has been removed. She cannot believe it: someone has taken him away! Was it not enough for him to be killed?

Our Mary runs away from the sepulcher stricken by the bitterest torment. She runs to rouse Simon Peter and John: "They've taken the Lord out of the tomb and we don't know where they've put him!" (Jn 20:2). While they hasten to verify her report, she gathers all her strength and returns to the tomb. "For where your treasure is, there will you heart be too," the Master had told them (Mt 6:21). Mary's heart is "in the garden" where the Master has been buried. But now the tomb is empty. Where is her treasure?

Mary is standing near the tomb crying. Suddenly she bends down to peer inside, "and saw two angels in white sitting where Jesus' body had been, one at the head and one at the feet" (Jn 20:12). The angels also see her and address her with the words used for the first time: "Woman, why are you weeping?"

Her response is immediate: "They've taken my Lord and I don't know where they've put him!" (Jn 20:13). Then, with a start, she turns around. Someone is standing right there. Lost in her sorrow, she does not raise her eyes; she is not interested in seeing the face of the new arrival who asks the same question: "Woman, why are you weeping?" and immediately adds: "Who are you looking for?" (Jn 20:15).

The final words are a sharp blow for Mary. Perhaps this man is in charge of the garden and he can be of more than the angels: "Sir, if you removed him, tell me where you put him and I'll take him away" (Jn 20:15). Again, she turns to look at the tomb. John plays on this multiple turning. Mary does not know how to take her eyes off the place where her treasure had been buried. However, something makes her "turn" suddenly and, in a new way, lift up her head: "Jesus said to her, 'Mary!' She turned and said to him, in Hebrew, 'Rabboni!' which means, 'Teacher!'" (Jn 20:16).

Mary's spinning around and her immediate recognition of the Master is splendid, and it is her amazement at hearing her name called that creates such splendor. He says, "Mary!" That unmistakable voice! There is such sweetness, such affection as he says her name that it touches her in the very depth of her being. Enchanted, Mary finds herself turned (in Greek: *strapheîsa*) toward the One who speaks her name. It is like a conversion, turning one's gaze from the past to the present, from the place where he was buried to the face of the Risen One!

Notice that Mary promptly exclaims in her native language, *Rabboni*, my Master! She has recognized the voice of the Good Shepherd who calls his lambs by name and leads them out (Jn 10:3)—out from their sorrows, from their obstinate focus on the past. She feels herself called by name. There are no doubts, the Lord is risen! Mary throws herself at the Master's feet and holds him in an affectionate embrace. We imagine her in this embrace based on John's text: "Stop touching me!" (not as sometimes translated: "Do not touch me!"). Mary must be embracing him if she is asked to "stop."

The new beginning

Why would Mary have to cease doing something as beautiful as embracing her adored Master? It is not certain why it becomes inappropriate. The Risen Lord does not despise heartfelt affection; he allows the women to express themselves with spontaneity and does not withdraw from their embrace. The evangelist Matthew attests to this in his account of the surprise appearance to the women who hurry from the sepulcher:

> And behold, Jesus met up with the women and said, "Hail!" They came forward, took hold of his feet, and worshipped him. (Mt 28:9)

Why then must Mary stop embracing the Master? Because, as Jesus explains, he must hurry to give the beautiful news to his disciples:

> Jesus said to her, "Don't hold on to me—I have not yet ascended to the Father. But go to my brothers and tell them, 'I am ascending to my Father and your Father, and to my God and your God.'" (Jn 20:17)

We find the same reason in the Gospel of Matthew. To the women who embrace his feet as they prostrate themselves in adoration, Jesus himself gives an extraordinarily important assignment:

> Then Jesus said to them, "Don't be afraid! Go tell my brothers to go to Galilee, and they will see me there." (Mt 28:10)

In both instances, Jesus calls the disciples "my brothers." The men who on the night of his passion abandoned him and left him in the hands of his enemies remain his "brothers." And Jesus, the risen Lord, sends to them Mary Magdalene and the other women who had faithfully followed him even to the foot of the cross and accompanied him to the tomb. The reward and joy of the first appearance are kept for these women.

∽ Toward Deeper Listening

In these two women who are in love with Christ, we can see an icon of the Christian vocation, in its fundamental dimension of passionate love for the person of Jesus.

John Paul II writes:

> From the beginning of Christ's mission, women show
> to him and to his mystery a *special sensitivity which is*
> *characteristic* of their *femininity*. It must also be said that
> this is especially confirmed in the Paschal Mystery, not
> only at the Cross but also at the dawn of the
> Resurrection. The women *are the first at the tomb*. They
> are the first to find it empty. They are the first to hear:
> "He is not here. *He has risen*, as he said" (Mt 28:6).
> They are the first to embrace his feet (cf. Mt 28:9).
> They are also the first to be called to announce this
> truth to the Apostles (cf. Mt 28:1–10; Lk 24:8–11).
> The Gospel of John (cf. also Mk 16:9) emphasizes *the*
> *special role of Mary Magdalene*. She is the first to meet
> the Risen Christ. At first she thinks he is the gardener;
> she recognizes him only when he calls her by name:
> "Jesus said to her, 'Mary.' She turned and said to him in
> Hebrew, 'Rabboni' (which means Teacher). Jesus said to
> her, 'Do not hold me, for I have not yet ascended to the
> Father, but go to my brethren and say to them, I am
> ascending to my Father and to your Father, to my God
> and your God.' Mary Magdalene went and said to the
> disciples, 'I have seen the Lord'; and she told them that
> he had said these things to her" (Jn 20:16–18).
>
> Hence she came to be called "the apostle of the
> Apostles." Mary Magdalene was the first eyewitness of
> the Risen Christ, and for this reason she was also *the*
> *first to bear witness to him before the Apostles*. This event,
> in a sense, crowns all that has been said previously
> about Christ entrusting divine truths to women as well
> as to men.[17]

∽ Biblical Texts

An anonymous woman, in Simon's house in Bethany, anoints Jesus' head with perfumed ointment: Mt 26:6–13; Mk 14:3–9.

The woman who is a sinner enters the house of Simon the Pharisee in Galilee and anoints with perfumed oil the feet of Jesus, bathing them with her tears and drying them with her hair: Lk 7:36–50.

Mary Magdalene evokes the image of the bride of the Song of Songs who after a long night of searching for her beloved once again finds him: Song 3:1–4; 5:2–8.

∽ Dialogue and Comparison

We now go from listening to meditation with the help of some questions. We allow ourselves to be personally summoned by the word, and we compare our life to Jesus Christ, the Word of the living God.

1. Mary of Bethany spared nothing: she poured out all of her precious perfume upon the Lord's feet. The measure of love is to give everything.

Do I allow myself to be conquered by this "logic of love"? Or do I pour out just enough perfume to appear generous and make a good impression?

2. As in the time of the disciples, so also today, there are people who protest certain forms of waste with apparently

sensible arguments. For example, it would be a waste of time to spend prolonged moments in prayer and adoration of the Lord—time that could be spent caring for the poor.

How would I answer this criticism? Do I grumble at other people who give everything? Am I afraid that God will ask me to give more than I can handle?

3. After the burial of Jesus, Mary Magdalene does not return home as do Peter and John. She stays near the tomb. She is the only one remaining in her persistent search for the Lord, like the bride of the Song of Songs who seeks the beloved of her heart. There are times when the Lord seems absent. The mystics speak of the "dark night of the soul," when God seems to completely disappear and we have to go in search of him.

Can I recall moments of darkness in my life when God seemed far away? How did I handle these moments?

What helps me to keep my search for the Lord alive?

4. Magdalene seeks "her Lord," but in the wrong places: at the tomb and among the dead. At times we can become attached to certain spiritual feelings and consolations of the past, to moments when we experienced the presence of the Lord. The encounter with the Risen One is prolonged in the joy of announcing him to others.

Do I allow the Risen One to guide me toward new horizons, or do I hold onto the past?

Do I express my faith and my love for Jesus Christ in the announcement of the Gospel in some service to the Church and in the witness of charity?

∞ Prayer

Let us contemplate the icon of these two disciples who are in love with the Lord and enliven within ourselves the love that first prompted us to follow Jesus Christ.

We ponder Mary of Bethany's act of pouring out the precious perfume over the Lord's feet. The one who loves spares nothing. We are also the objects of waste from God's point of view. He lavishes on us all the perfumed oil of his love: "you anoint my head with oil, my cup overflows" (Ps 23:5).

We contemplate Mary Magdalene at the feet of the Risen One, her rushing to bring the joyful announcement to the community of the disciples. We entrust to her, "the apostle to the Apostles," our commitment to joyful evangelization.

We pray together:

Response: *Make us witnesses of your resurrection, Lord!*

Considering the example of Mary Magdalene, we ask to undertake the journey of conversion and the following of Jesus Christ with dedication, we pray: R.

May the Lord grant us the ability to hear his voice calling us by name, as did Mary of Magdala on Easter morning, and may we encounter him as the Living One, we pray: R.

For our communities, that like Mary Magdalene they may announce the resurrection so that we may know how to give the witness of paschal joy, we pray: R.

Holy Father, we thank you through Jesus Christ your Son, risen from the dead in the power of the Holy Spirit. Teach us to recognize the signs of the resurrection in the events of our lives and give us the gift of a renewed thrust in announcing the victory of Christ over death. Amen.

———•◆•———

We entrust to the Virgin Mary, Mother of hope, our resolution to place ourselves at the service of the Church's missionary efforts.

Chapter 16

The Hour of "the Woman":
From Cana to Revelation

At the beginning of our New Testament journey, we contemplated the "here I am" of Mary, her yes. Mary is the woman of faith, "she who believed," as Elizabeth indicates in her greeting (Lk 1:45).

Now, following the steps of the fourth evangelist, we will see Mary as the mother of believers, who teaches us to listen and to do what Jesus says.

John presents Mary above all as the Mother who at Cana opens the way for the hour of the messianic revelation of Jesus: "Jesus did this, the first of his signs, at Cana in Galilee and revealed his glory, and his disciples believed in him" (Jn. 2:11).

In the intimacy of the cenacle, the Master prepares his disciples for the recognition of his and their "hour." The image that spontaneously surfaces is that of the woman when she arrives at "her hour" (Jn 16:21).

Here she is, the mother of the Lord at the foot of the cross, present with her whole being at the death of the Son, which will bring forth the birth of the Church. It is her *hour:* "Woman, here is your son" (Jn 19:26).

John never calls Mary by her name, but rather he uses the title "Woman." This title ideally links the Mother of Christ to the first woman of Genesis and the woman in Revelation who gives birth to a son destined to govern all nations (cf. Rev 12:5).

The woman's hour has not yet come to completion. Revelation presents the striking image of the woman clothed with the sun, with the moon under her feet and a crown of twelve stars on her head, but who suffers the pains of labor (Rev 12:1–6). The Church, already a participant in the victory of her Lord, is called to give birth to a new humanity.

We invoke the Creator Spirit, who makes all things new, to reinvigorate our hearts and make us capable of persevering anticipation. The Spirit and the Bride say: "Come." Yes, all creation groans and invokes you: Come, Lord Jesus!

☞ LISTENING

At Cana, the first of the signs

We place ourselves at Cana in the joyous climate of a wedding feast (see Jn 2:1–11) the day before Passover. The traditional site is Kefr Kenna, a little more than six miles northeast of Nazareth.

The evangelist introduces the story by indicating a measure of time: "On the third day" (Jn 2:1). The third day is the preferred time for great "signs" and alludes to the resurrection (cf. Jn 2:19; 4:43; 11:6).

"The mother of Jesus was there." Mary is the first person introduced; she is a critical figure in the unfolding of the passage, as she will be at the foot of the cross. Again, John never calls her by her name (2:12; 19:25); here she is referred to as "the mother of," a title of honor.

"Now Jesus and his disciples had also been invited to the wedding" (Jn 2:2)—by now Jesus and his disciples have become a stable group, so when he is invited to the wedding, they go along.

The account unfolds then in the following sequence:

- The dialogue between the mother and Jesus (v. 3–5).
- The central theme of Jesus giving wine in abundance (v. 6–8).
- The head waiter's careful consideration (v. 9–10).
- The summarizing conclusion (v. 11).

We linger over Mary's words, nine in all: four addressed to her son and six to the servants. Mary says to Jesus: *Oínon ouch 'échousin*, "they have no wine." These words express simultaneously her observation of the problem and her desire to ease the embarrassment. She has full confidence that Jesus will resolve the situation positively. Wine, the type used in connection with a nuptial banquet, already has strong symbolic meaning in the Old Testament: it is a sign of salvation and of the magnificence of the messianic era.

However, Jesus seems to shield and distance himself from Mary's request. His words seem harsh. The phrase "What do you want from me, woman?" (Jn 2:4) comes from an original colloquial Hebraic expression. The precise significance of the words depends on the concrete circumstance. In this case, it seems to highlight the diverse positions on the matter in question: the shortage of wine.

> Jesus seems to want to point out his position and that of his mother in relation to the two levels of meaning that the wine has. Mary is preoccupied with the material wine of the wedding; Jesus has in mind the symbolic wine of the messianic time.[18]

The wine Jesus has in mind is associated with his "hour," therefore the culmination of his mission, the hour of his passion and glorification.

Mary does not reply, nor does she stop to clarify the meaning of her son's words. With great calm and confidence, she turns to the servants: "Do whatever he tells you" (Jn 2:5). The phrase repeats the command Pharaoh gave the Egyptians at the beginning of seven years of famine: "Go to Joseph; what he says to you, do" (Gen 41:55). Here we see clearly emerging the mediatory role of the Mother of Jesus. She presents to her Son the situation of need, our "wine shortage," and instructs the servants, the Church, in the necessary attitude: "Do whatever he tells you." The rest will follow as a consequence. But what comes as a surprise, a marvel, is the extraordinarily good and superabundant wine! The quality is such that the expert, "the head steward of the table," is left speechless.

At Cana, Mary reveals to us who her Son really is. Her prompting coincides with that of the Baptist in the following chapter: Jesus is the Messiah, the bridegroom, he who "gives the Spirit without measure" (Jn 3:34).

The first sign Jesus performs through the intercession of his mother symbolically foreshadows the hour of the great messianic marriage, it manifests the glory of Christ, and it brings to faith his first disciples, the seeds of the Church.

Golgotha: from sign to reality

We place ourselves spiritually at Calvary, " 'The Place of the Skull,' in Hebrew, Golgotha" (Jn 19:17). It is the hour of death and the definitive hour of Jesus' true glory. He is hung on the wood of the cross as a criminal, but John describes him as a king, holding the key position. He is the true messianic king:

> [W]here they crucified him and with him two others, on either side, while Jesus was in the middle. (Jn 19:18)

He who had begun his public life transforming water into wine now completes th´yat sign by giving his own life, his Spirit. But life always germinates in a mother's womb, and here is his mother at the foot of the cross. At Cana she anticipated the revelation of his glory, and now she stands on Calvary. She says nothing. She keeps everything in her heart so as not to add to her son's pain.

Now her dying son takes the initiative to speak words including the article, *Gýnai, íde ho hyios sou*, "Woman, here is your son." Then he turns to the beloved disciple: "Here is your mother" (Jn 19:26–27).

The first of these words is "woman," which seems out of place coming from the mouth of a dying son. But it is not out of place coming from the mouth of the Messiah, who is revealing a profound truth: the new motherhood of Mary, which corresponds to the motherhood of the first woman, "the mother of all living" (Gen 3:20).

The expression, "here is your son," joined to the corresponding, "here is your mother," establishes a mother-son relationship between Mary and John. And it is important that this relationship is established precisely as the Messiah is dying. He himself establishes his mother in a role of spiritual, messianic motherhood. From that hour forward, Mary is no longer only "the mother of Jesus" but also the mother of John and of all believers, represented by the beloved disciple.

The woman gives birth in pain

The text of John 16:21–23 forms a hinge between the two passages that we have meditated on up to this point. The image of the woman in labor becomes a model for the situation of trial (the hour of the disciples) and the hermeneutical key for Christ's own hour, that of the Paschal Mystery.

There seems to be a link between the image of the woman in labor and the woman-mother at the side of Jesus' cross, a connection grasped by John Paul II in *Mulieris Dignitatem:*

"When a woman is in travail she has sorrow, because her hour has come; but when she is delivered of the child, *she no longer remembers the anguish*, for joy that a child is born into the world" (Jn 16:21). The first part of Christ's words refers to the "pangs of childbirth," which belong to the heritage of original sin; at the same time these words indicate *the link that exists between the woman's motherhood and the Paschal Mystery*. For this mystery also includes the Mother's sorrow at the foot of the Cross—the Mother who through faith shares in the amazing mystery of her Son's "self-emptying": "This is perhaps the deepest 'kenosis' of faith in human history."

As we contemplate this Mother, whose heart "a sword has pierced" (cf. Lk 2:35), our thoughts go *to all the suffering women in the world*, suffering either physically or morally. In this suffering a woman's sensitivity plays a role, even though she often succeeds in resisting suffering better than a man....

But the words of the Gospel about the woman who suffers when the time comes for her to give birth to her child, immediately afterwards express joy: it is *"the joy that a child is born into the world."* This joy too is referred to the Paschal Mystery, to the joy which is communicated to the Apostles on *the day of Christ's Resurrection.*[19]

The woman about to give birth in Revelation

The image of the woman giving birth returns in the final book of the Bible, Revelation. Here is a type of the ideal woman, the firstborn, in all her splendor and sovereignty: "a woman clothed with the sun, with the moon beneath her feet and a crown of twelve stars on her head" (Rev 12:1). From her womb comes the ideal Son, who has been kept close to God and who now descends so he can do battle on earth. Who is this woman? Israel, Mary, the Church? Rather than being clear and distinct, the author of Revelation uses images and figures. It is a little like a game of mirrors: one image leads to another, always calling one further.

There is *heaven*, which is the space of God. There we find the woman, but also the furious dragon. There we find that Michael, who struggles against the dragon, defeats him, and sends him plummeting to the earth (see Rev 12:7–9). The *earth* is the space of men, women, and history. The woman's earthly descendents fight and are persecuted by the dragon, the serpent of old. And finally there is the *sea*, the symbolic place of primordial chaos and evil power: "The dragon was enraged with the woman and went off to wage war against the rest of her offspring—those who keep God's commandments and accept the testimony of Jesus. And he stood on the sands of the sea" (Rev 12:17–18).

This woman, with whom the dragon is infuriated, has already given birth, and her son is safe beside God. Yet the woman must again give birth and struggle. She is the new Zion, symbolized as a woman in her eschatological maternity. She is the new Jerusalem that descends from heaven in order to regenerate the earthly Jerusalem:

> Christ, with his values, is already present and alive in his Church. These are the "holdings" that the pregnant woman-church possesses and must express in the con-

creteness of her history, making herself grow and develop those values of Christ of which she is the carrier.[20]

∽ TOWARD DEEPER LISTENING

The woman-church cannot be freed from the pains of labor. She must live her hour in the certainty that as soon as her child is born, "she will no longer remember her suffering...." "So you, too," concludes the Lord. "I'll see you again and your hearts will rejoice, and no one will take your joy from you" (Jn 16:21–22).

John Paul II writes:

> [I]n the face of the "mighty works of God" ... Saint Paul, as a man, feels the need to refer to what is essentially feminine in order to express the truth about his own apostolic service. This is exactly what Paul of Tarsus does when he addresses the Galatians with the words: "My little children, with whom I am again in travail" (Gal 4:19)....
>
> The Council has confirmed that, unless one looks to the Mother of God, it is impossible to understand the mystery of the Church, her reality, her essential vitality.[21]

∽ BIBLICAL TEXTS

The prophetic word of Simeon to the mother of Jesus: "And a sword will pierce your own soul," Lk 2:35.

"All creation has been groaning in labor pains," Rom 8:18–25.

"As soon as Zion was in labor she delivered her children," Isa 66:7–13.

"The Spirit and the Bride say, 'Come!'" Rev 22:17–20.

ᗧ DIALOGUE AND COMPARISON

We now go from listening to meditation with the help of some questions. We allow ourselves to be personally summoned by the word, and we compare our life to Jesus Christ, the Word of the living God.

1. At Cana, Mary reveals not only Jesus, but also herself. She is indeed the woman who is attentive to the situation, with her eyes and heart open to the needs of others and, even more, with the knowledge of whom to turn to in order to resolve the problem.

Do I turn to Mary in my difficulties? Do I value her intercession with her Son?

Do I allow Mary, who reminds me, "Do whatever he tells you," to guide me?

2. On the cross, Jesus reveals himself as the Good Shepherd who gives his life for his sheep. Mary, fully associated to his offering, accepts from him the gift of motherhood of the Church: "Woman, here is your son."

How have I, like the beloved disciple, allowed Mary into "my dwelling"?

How do I accept moments of suffering and difficulty?

How do I accept the sacrifices necessary to bring to birth in faith those entrusted to me by God?

3. In the attitude of waiting for the fulfillment of salvation, the word of God invites us to responsibility. Our Church is called to the marvelous work of bringing Christ and his values to birth once again in this third millennium.

Am I a living member of this Church?

Do I make an effort, in this birthing of a new humanity, to go out of myself and my comfort zone?

What can I concretely do in my parish to renew and infuse hope in those who have lost it: the young, the lonely, the elderly, the sick, and others?

⌒ Prayer

Let us contemplate the icon of Mary at Cana—we present to the Lord, through the intercession of Mary, the needs of which we are aware.

Let us contemplate the icon of Mary on Calvary—we entrust to the Sorrowful Mother of the Lord the sorrows of humanity and in particular the women who continue her passion today, standing beneath other crosses. We pray together:

> *Mother of the Word*
> *accept with love whoever turns to you,*
> *you who mercifully guide to fertile pastures*
> *the flock redeemed by your Son*
> *who was born of you.*
> *Save the poor people who beg you*
> *to guard and defend them*
> *that they may joyfully carry*

the sweet yoke of the Gospel.
Let us contemplate the icon of the radiant woman of
Revelation—let us reawaken our hope and our lively
expectation of the reign of God.
In communion with our brothers and sisters in the faith,
we greet Mary:
"Ave, you who bring forth joy.
Ave, you who destroy sorrow.
Ave, you who scatter the clouds from souls,
illuminating them with spiritual splendors.
These are the souls who, with faith and fervor,
sing to you,
Mother of God."

———•◆•———

We entrust to Mary, mother at Cana and on Calvary, our resolution to be ever more aware of the needs of those around us and to grow in our willingness to share in some way in the sufferings of others.

Notes

Part I: Women in the Old Testament

1. John Paul II, *Mulieris Dignitatem*, no. 6.

2. Gerhard von Rad, *Genesis* (Philadelphia: Westminster Press, 1972).

3. Ibid., 119.

4. Melkhilta Ex 13:19 (the halakic midrash to the Book of Exodus).

5. James Alberione, *Sermons to the Sisters of Jesus, the Good Shepherd*, vol. I (Rome: Edizioni Paoline, 1961), 16.

6. A. Niccacci, *The House of Wisdom* (Milan: Cinisello Balsamo, 1994), 50.

7. E. Bosetti, *La tenda e il bastione* (Milan: Cinisello Balsamo, 1992), 134.

8. Saint Teresa of Avila, *Thoughts on the Love of God*, IV, 7: *Works* (Rome: 1992), 1012.

Part II: Women in the New Testament

1. "Le Livre de la Genèse," in A. Malet, P. Marcel, M. Rèveillaud, *Commentaires de Jean Calvin sure l'Ancien Testament*, I, (Geneva: 1961), 527.

2. Martin Luther, *Enarrationes in Genesin* [Lectures on Genesis], WA 44, 314.

3. Vatican Council II, *Lumen Gentium*, no. 55.

4. Pope John Paul II, General Audience of July 24, 1996.

5. *Mulieris Dignitatem*, no. 17.

6. Saint Clement of Alexandria, *Paedagogus* [*The Instructor*], I, 6, 421.

7. Saint Augustine, Sermon 192, *In Natale Domini* IX, 2; *PL* 46, 937–938.

8. Saint Bede, *Explanation of the Apocalypse*, II; *PL* 93, 166.

9. *Lumen Gentium*, no. 55.

10. Heinz Schürmann, *Il vangelo di Luca*, CTNT 3/1 (Brescia: Paideai, 1983), 434.

11. The Italian word, *"Maestro"* may be translated as either *Teacher* or *Master*. In this text we have preferred the term *Master* as a way of underscoring Jesus' identity as the Master of Life who forms us to his way of life and who calls all Christians to a profound master/disciple relationship. *Trans.*

12. Saint Irenaeus, *Against Heresies*, IV, 20:5–7.

13. Saint Augustine, *Tractates on the Gospel of John, 15:10–12.*

14. For the history of this image, refer to: Ricci, Carla; Paul Burns, trans. *Mary Magdalene and Many Others: Women Who Followed Jesus* (Minneapolis, MN: Fortress Press, 1994), pp. 32–55.

15. Ibid.

16. Pope John Paul II, *Vita Consecrata*, no. 94.

17. *Mulieris Dignitatem*, no. 16.

18. A. Niccacci, *Il vangelo oggi* (Assisi, 1979), 28.

19. *Mulieris Dignitatem*, no. 19.

20. Ugo Vanni, *L'Apocalisse* (Bologna: EDB, 1988), 345.

21. *Mulieris Dignitatem*, no. 22.

Bibliography

Adinolfi, M. *Il femminismo della Bibbia* (Rome: Antonianum, 1981).

Aubert, J. M. *La donna: Antifemminismo e cristianesimo* (Assisi: Cittadella, 1976).

_____. *Le donne dicono Dio* (Milan: Edizioni Paoline, 1995).

Bonora, A. (ed.). "Debora, Rut, Giuditta e Ester" in *La spiritualità dell'Antico Testamento* (Bologna: EDB, 1987).

Bosetti, E. "Donne nella Bibbia: vie diverse alla pace," RTM 28 (1995), 341–348; *Canto di pace: la donna nella Bibbia*, CSV, (Castel Gandolfo [RM], 1996).

Fabris, R., and V. Gozzini, *La donna nell'esperienza della prima chiesa* (Rome: Edizioni Paoline, 1982).

Grelot, P. *La donna nel Nuovo Testamento* (Milan: San Paolo, Cinisello Balsamo, 1996).

Malet, A., Marcel, P., Rèveillaud. *Commentaires de Jean Calvin sur L'Ancien Testament, I* (Gèneve: 1961).

Ricci, C. *Maria di Magdala e le molte altre: Donne sul cammino di Gesù* (Naples: D'Auria, 1991).

Rigato, M. L. "Donne testimoni della Risurrezione," in *Uomini e donne nella chiesa*. Edited by S. Spera (Rome: 1988), 37–53.

Schüssler Fiorenza, E. *In Memory of Her: A Feminist Theological Reconstruction of Christian Origins* (New York: Crossroads, 1983).

Sebastiani, L. *Donne dei vangeli: Tratti personali e teologici* (Milan: Edizioni Paoline, 1994).

Vanni, Ugo. *L'Apocalisse* (Bologna: EDB, 1988).

Von Rad, Gerhard. *Genesis: A Commentary* (Louisville, KY: Westminster/John Knox Press, 1973).

BOOKS & MEDIA

A mission of the Daughters of St. Paul

As apostles of Jesus Christ, evangelizing today's world:

We are CALLED to holiness
by God's living Word and Eucharist.

We COMMUNICATE the Gospel message
through our lives and through all
available forms of media.

We SERVE the Church
by responding to the hopes and needs
of all people with the Word of God,
in the spirit of St. Paul.

For more information visit our website:
www.pauline.org.

BOOKS & MEDIA

The Daughters of St. Paul operate book and media centers at the following addresses. Visit, call or write the one nearest you today, or find us on the World Wide Web, www.pauline.org

CALIFORNIA
3908 Sepulveda Blvd, Culver City, CA 90230 — 310-397-8676
2640 Broadway Street, Redwood City, CA 94063 — 650-369-4230
5945 Balboa Avenue, San Diego, CA 92111 — 858-565-9181

FLORIDA
145 S.W. 107th Avenue, Miami, FL 33174 — 305-559-6715

HAWAII
1143 Bishop Street, Honolulu, HI 96813 — 808-521-2731
Neighbor Islands call: — 866-521-2731

ILLINOIS
172 North Michigan Avenue, Chicago, IL 60601 — 312-346-4228

LOUISIANA
4403 Veterans Memorial Blvd, Metairie, LA 70006 — 504-887-7631

MASSACHUSETTS
885 Providence Hwy, Dedham, MA 02026 — 781-326-5385

MISSOURI
9804 Watson Road, St. Louis, MO 63126 — 314-965-3512

NEW JERSEY
561 U.S. Route 1, Wick Plaza, Edison, NJ 08817 — 732-572-1200

NEW YORK
150 East 52nd Street, New York, NY 10022 — 212-754-1110

PENNSYLVANIA
9171-A Roosevelt Blvd, Philadelphia, PA 19114 — 215-676-9494

SOUTH CAROLINA
243 King Street, Charleston, SC 29401 — 843-577-0175

VIRGINIA
1025 King Street, Alexandria, VA 22314 — 703-549-3806

CANADA
3022 Dufferin Street, Toronto, ON M6B 3T5 — 416-781-9131

¡También somos su fuente para libros,
videos y música en español!